ONE
Percent

AUTHORED BY

RAY E. THOMPSON, SR. AND
LYRAE D. NELSON-THOMPSON

ISBN: 978-1-64314-296-8 (Paperback)
        978-1-64314-297-5 (Hardback)
        978-1-64314-298-2 (Ebook)

AuthorsPress
California, USA
www.authorspress.com

CONTENTS

ACKNOWLEDGMENTS

This book is dedicated to my incredible wife and life-long partner, LyRae D. Nelson-Thompson, **who was also my co-author**, along with my two awesome children, Ray E. Thompson, Jr. and Son'Serae A. Thompson. In addition to these important people in my life I must include my Mother, Elsie M. Thompson. To the memory of my father, Reverend Albert A. Thompson, and my grandmother in-love, Mrs. Barbara G. Nelson. As I travel the roads of my mind, I must remember the following individuals: James and Carolyn, Angeline and Valentine, Pastor Stephen, Evangeline and James, Roger and Lynette, Roger II, Jackie, Kim, Joyce and Earl, Danny, Ray and Sharon, Rodney (Best Friend), Glen (Best Friend), Christopher (Best Friend) and Gale, Debra, Pastor Scottie and Regina. I also thank God for all of those that sent flowers, cards, and gifts. For all those who called, texted and most of all prayed.

CHAPTER 1

AT FIRST SIGHT

I am forty-eight years old. I lived my life the best I could. I learned the hard way, and most importantly, I loved fiercely.

I have been lying in this hospital bed for days, with nothing to look at but the ceiling. It looks different today.

Am I tilting my head a little too much to the right?

How long has that crack been there?

Did it appear when I was sleeping?

Was I even asleep?

I cannot tell anymore.

My eyes betray me.

The only thing in this room that gives me comfort is the sound of the heater. It never changes. From the time I got here to the time I am in now, whatever it may be, it remains a vibrating but soothing constant.

You see, I have been healthy for the most part. I would not call myself athletic, but I would not call me lazy either. I am your typical try guy—to say the least.

Being here, in this hospital, is something I never thought would happen to me. If you are someone who's not used to being in a cramped space with tubes inside you, then you'll know what I am talking about. It is the little things you see that you tend to amplify.

A nurse is here, checking my vitals. As a part of what seems to be a routine line of questioning, she asks, "Do you know who the president is?"

I nod to confirm. "It is President Trump."

"And do you know what date it is?"

I try to recall the last few days. It has been hazy, but I know. "It is the thirty-first of January 2017."

"Do you know where you are?"

"I am at WellSpan York Hospital, in York, Pennsylvania."

"Very good," she says as she types some information into the laptop. She pushes the laptop and its platform over to the side, gives me a quick smile, and leaves.

I follow her with my gaze toward the door. I cannot help but notice the empty chairs on the sides.

Has it been that long since the last time I was in a room full of kind and loving people?

Has it been that long since my last homemade meal?

Where has everyone gone to?

I have been so tired lately, any extra movements, and talking, just exhausts me. Even the nonthreatening effort of thinking takes a toll on me. As I watch the nurse leave, I feel myself start to drift in and out of consciousness. They say that before you pass, your life flashes before your eyes like a movie—a silver screen of memories. I breathe in, breathe out, and let the film roll.

*****

Once again, it was 1986, and I was two weeks in as a freshman at Howard University, Washington, D. C. It was a warm day in August, and I was on the Yard walking rather aimlessly when an overwhelming feeling washes over me. I looked around at this large expanse of grass and trees, and I knew that I was standing on hallowed ground. A lot of memories have been made here, and I was going to make a few of my own.

I found myself in front of the Fine Arts building. As I looked up, I saw a young lady. She was weaving through a sea of students coming toward me. It seemed to me that she too was wandering around, just like I was. She ended up stopping in front of me. I thought she looked familiar when we locked eyes. I was not sure whether I met her before or if I had seen her around campus. I thought about it for a second, and I realized that I saw her during registration. She was in the same line. She had a "Don't I know you?" look on her face when she saw me, and so I decided to strike up a conversation.

"Hey, didn't I see you in the registration line?"

"Yes! That is why you look so familiar! I am Felicia, nice to meet you," she replied.

I said to her, "My name is Ray, nice to formally meet you."

We were both freshmen. I learned that Felicia, like me, was from New Jersey. We had a great conversation. We talked a lot about where we grew up. Eventually, I asked her what brought her to Howard University. She told me it was the prestige and the legacy. She was inspired by the many prominent African Americans who went to Howard and that was what brought her to the school. Before I could ask her who inspired her the most, she asked me the same question.

"What brought you to Howard University?" she asked.

Without hesitation, I replied, "I came here to find a wife."

She paused, her eyebrows shot up, and her eyes grew wide. She was startled by that. Then her eyes narrowed. "What do you mean?" she asked curiously.

"Well, secondary, I am here for an education. My primary goal is to find a wife," I told her.

"Well, what kind of woman are you looking for?"

"The young lady that I came to look for is no taller than five feet two inches. She is on the quiet side and very ladylike. She has a darker skin complexion, a well-rounded and sweet individual."

"That is kind of funny!" she said, amused.

"What do you mean?" I asked.

"It is a little bizarre," she said and laughed again. "I have two roommates, and you just described one of them."

I did not expect that. I was totally shocked. "I would like to meet your roommate," I said to her then.

"Here she is now," she said as she nodded toward the person approaching us. "Dee! Over here." She waved Dee over.

I was surprised and confused that the young lady I was looking at was six feet tall and fair skinned. As Dee approached us, I saw that she was approaching with another young lady.

"Ray, these are my roommates Dee," Felicia said, gesturing toward the tall girl, "and LyRae," referring to the young lady who was hidden from my view until then.

LyRae.

The person who was standing before me was exactly the person I had just described as my future wife. She was the one, and I knew it instantly. It was as if God was telling me, "This is your wife, LyRae." It was about seventy-eight degrees outside, normal for that time of year. She was dressed in sensible clothing. She donned shorts, a simple T-shirt, and sandals. She was prim and proper, very lady-like. She carried herself in a way that made you want to address her as "Ma'am." She seemed like she was very much in control of herself, even in chaotic situations, like she always maintained a level head.

"Hello," was all I could muster. I could not say anything. I was awestruck.

"Hello," Dee and LyRae replied politely.

They told Felicia they were heading to Crampton Auditorium and went on their way. Felicia and I continued with our conversation as LyRae and Dee walked away.

"When you go back to your room and you see LyRae, tell her that she is the woman I came to Howard University to marry," I said to Felicia.

She smiled and shook her head. "All right, I will."

She later told me that LyRae was not interested in me, or in anyone else, that she came to Howard to receive an education and after that she planned to return to New Jersey since she too was from New Jersey; but that did not faze me.

In the following months, I became very good friends with both Dee and Felicia and the both of them helped me grow closer to LyRae. Dee and Felicia would give me intel to wherever she was, and I would go wherever she would be. I would constantly show up in places like the cafeteria, Burr gym, or the bookstore; but most of the time, she would be in the undergraduate library reading books related to her studies and she would catch me looking at her. We would talk, and I would ask her out for lunch or dinner.

She always said no.

Despite her constant rejections and me feeling bad about myself, I never gave up on her. I knew she was the one for me. I had a feeling of certainty that she was the one. It just felt true.

I wanted her.

I needed her.

I was in love with her.

I will marry her. I will go home to her every single day for the rest of my life, in sickness and in health. She is the one who will nag at me to take out the trash, or replace the toilet paper rolls, or put the cap back on the toothpaste. She is the one who will raise my children with me. I just knew.

I kept pursuing her. I never wavered.

One day I beat her to the undergraduate library. I knew she was on her way. I did the exact same thing I did every day. "Would you like to go on a date with me?"

"Sure," she said.

"All right," and I started walking away. Wait a second. Did she just say yes? "Did you just say yes?"

"Yes." She giggled.

I was elated. "I will pick you up at seven." I left quickly before she could change her mind.

She finally agreed to go out on a date with me. I could not believe it! I wondered what made her say yes this time. She probably thought that if she gave me the date that I have been asking for months, I would stop. And well, she knew it happened to be my birthday that day. It could have been that. I smiled to myself and walked back to my dorm to get ready.

I started getting nervous. I was nervous. I did not want to say the wrong thing or do anything to upset her.

I picked her up at seven o'clock sharp, and we took a taxi. She looked beautiful that night. Her makeup was flawless. Her hair was down and combed around her face, the style that emphasizes her bone structure and the color of her eyes. Her clothes were matched perfectly, and she wore three-inch heels that complemented her attire.

I could not take my eyes off her. Every now and then I would do something clumsy that would make her laugh. I did not care. I liked seeing her laugh. Everything about her made me happy.

Since it was my birthday, she decided to take me out instead. So she took me to a place called Unos in Georgetown, about fifteen miles away from the university. It was a popular place back then. The place was packed, but I did not see anyone from Howard that night. We took one of the booths and shared their famous pepperoni pizza.

My detective work checked out. She was a psychology major and hailed from a rural place in New Jersey called Swedesboro. The more I got to know her, the more I wanted her close to me. She was smart and mature for her age. On top of that, I knew in an instant that she had a heart gilded with kindness, never mean or cruel, but polite and compassionate. I wanted to know everything about her, what she thought, how she felt.

It was like a hunger, and my stomach was a bottomless pit.

She told me how she did not believe in dating, and I told her that if she just gave me a chance, I was absolutely sure we could have a nice relationship and that she would never date anyone else in life.

"You know, you scared me for a bit there. I thought you were some psycho stalker. I told my dad about you."

I laughed nervously. "In what context? Were you bragging about me?" I let out a subdued chuckle.

"Well, your attempts at getting my attention, though methodical, were less than charming. It was more of telling my dad a joke rather than bragging."

"If talking about me brings a smile to your face, I would say being a joke is not half bad."

She gave me a wry smile.

I continued, "So what did he have to say?"

"Oh, he just reminded me that I have cousins in the area who would not mind meeting you."

The sudden progression of where this conversation was going hit me like a football to the face.

I was shocked and, to be honest, a little scared.

I told her, "I am not ready to meet your family just yet, but if you give me more time, I could—"

She cuts me off by saying, "Before you say anything ambitious, I just want to make things clear. These cousins of mine are more of a"—she paused—"a contingency if at any point this all goes south."

"How do I reassure you that I do not mean any harm?"

"You could start off by dropping the smooth talking and just, I do not know, be you? All I see is some guy who cannot take no for an answer. I need to know if there's more to you. I just need to get to know you."

Then it struck me. I did not come off as that modern-day Casanova my mind has shaped my self-image to be. I came off to her as Arthur Richard Jackson, a stalker. I ran a mental checklist in my head to see where I went wrong.

Flowers? Uncheck. Those things are more expensive than how they are portrayed in movies.

Chocolates? Uncheck. What if she is diabetic?

Love letters? Uncheck. I could write a paper about angular momentum in respect to how the room seems to spin before I have the guts to talk to her, but that would've just landed in the trash bin.

I was dumbfounded, with a whirlwind of questions in my head, trying to challenge her skewed notion about me; but the only question that escaped my lips for that moment were . . .

"Where do I start?"

Where do I start? Is that all I could come up with? I had more to say, more to prove that I was not someone to be scared of; but at the same time, I felt those were the words she wanted to hear, words that allowed myself to be vulnerable, just like how she was every time I followed her around.

She looked down at her slice of pizza for a brief pause, and she slid her gaze back to me.

"Did you really understand that book about behaviorism while you waited for me in the library, or was that your desperate attempt to impress me?"

As if on cue, we broke into a fit of laughter and that night marked the first night of our being inseparable.

There were nights when LyRae would get these random cravings for a chocolate milkshake from McDonald's, which was some distance from the university. I did not want her walking alone late at night; so I'd walk twenty minutes from Drew Hall, past the Green Memorial Stadium and the Mcmillan Reservoir, past the Yard, and all the way to Tubman Quad, plus another twenty minutes to McDonald's to spend five minutes with her and get that milkshake with her.

I enjoyed every second of it. Then I would walk back to Drew Hall. At that point, I knew LyRae was safe.

Some days we spend on the school grounds. Bags plopped like huge rocks on long manicured grass. She loves making these tiny sandwiches with super thick slices of ham and copious amount of cheddar, ready to burst at the first bite.

But the real takeaways are the juice boxes. They remind me of home. Some people want sunflowers in summer. Others look up for snowflakes in winter. Most go to great lengths just to catch that first hint of warmth after long days of cold. People always seem to find meaning in what is about to begin.

What I have with her, I know I will never have it any other way. To me, she was a beginning I never wish to end.

Some nights we would wait outside until the sun comes up.

She called me to her dorm one night. It was one of those quiet Sundays where we would usually sit on top of the undergraduate library and just stare at the view. The last round of calm before the manic immediacy of Monday.

"Look how the stars just disappeared like that," she said, just a few seconds after dawn.

"That is what happens when you let too much light in."

"When it is too bright, the rest just blurs in the background. It is like an entire universe gets hidden," I said.

She turned to me.

I traced the morning light on her face and said, "I must say, you are particularly radiant today. More than the usual. It is like you are glowing."

"It is the sun making you see all sorts of things not there," she replied with a shy schoolgirl grin.

"You are getting better at this."

"With what?"

"Talking your way out of a compliment."

Another smile and she disappeared into her room.

It was one of those moments that I remember where I pinch myself and ask,

How can anyone be this happy?

How can anyone be as bad at this as I am?

How can any of this be real?

It is just not possible.

Although it was clear to everyone we knew that we were a couple, for the most part, LyRae and I were great friends. Our sort of friendship was reaching a point where we saw the world in the same perspective. The pace in which our thoughts raced with one another defeated the need for words.

Sure, we had our little fights every now and then. Like whose turn it is to pick the movie we were to watch or the dinner we were to grab afterward.

Or how her anger flies off the handle sometimes when she catches me spacing out in the middle of her full-blown discussion on constructivist theories.

How can something so tiny-bodied release that amount of intensity? For the life of me, it is something I will never be able to answer. But it is a depth I am willing to spend a lifetime to explore.

Four years flew by quickly, and during that time, she grew from her challenges and I bore witness to how these events refined her both in mind and heart. As I watched her grow into this amazing woman, I could not help but notice that I too grew with her. I felt better about myself, and even more so just being with her. My love was sewn with both admiration and deeper respect.

As graduation approached, I thought of my future and how I just could not picture my life without LyRae.

I yearned to be her provider.

I wished to be her protector.

I dreamed of loving her without rest.

My mind leaped into the future as these wholehearted aspirations took shape in the form of a family I felt was mine. I saw where I wanted to be.

I saw this while I was standing, of all places, in front of a fruit stand. This one overwhelmingly red apple somehow stood out. How many times have I seen one? Hundreds. Maybe thousands of the same, in my entire fruit-eating existence. But I know, in my gut, as I do the math in my head, that I could be wrong.

Because I have never actually seen an apple before. Not once. Not truly. Really seeing takes more. I found myself regarding the same apple as if in a trance. Temporarily possessed by some form of maddening compulsion. Observing where the shadows fall. Reaching out and feeling its every curve. Turning it around. Taking a bite. Imagining the sunlight absorbed in it—conjuring up scenes of its beginnings.

When I saw LyRae that day, it was almost the same kind of stirring. I saw her and felt something was about to unravel within me. Like water gathering in spring, before it flows, before it starts to find its ways through the streams. I saw what was going to happen to me before it did. Before anyone could. A glimpse of a secret universe from the outside looking in, waiting.

I knew that hers was the only love I wanted. I wanted to marry her so that I could fully express my love for her and be right in the eyes of our Lord.

And I wanted to set an example for our future children—show them what real love looks like.

I knew that it was the time to set the wheels of our destiny in motion. With all this in mind, I sought out to secure a lifetime's promise. I was intent on buying her a ring, but that was just the easy part.

I nervously phoned her mother to ask permission for LyRae's hand in marriage.

Her mother, Mrs. Jackie, is quite the character. She stood at a height of five feet and four inches. She had a mane of dark-brown hair that brings out her eyes. Her dark-brown eyes, having seen a cycle of peace and war, were shielded by glasses. She was in her late thirties at the time.

Although she may pass off as your average, harmless-looking, friendly neighbor, her words betrayed any attempts at subtlety, showcasing a direct link between her mind and her mouth.

Just imagine if a thunder ever tried to keep down its roar behind the clouds—she would be the earthling equivalent.

Nothing from what she shows on the seemingly delicate outside could ever hold back anything she may be simmering within.

The thought of asking for her daughter's hand in marriage from a person like her is intimidating, to say the least.

With each interval of the ringing sound of my unanswered call, I not only contemplated about what to say but also agonized over how to say it.

Should I take a direct approach?

Good morning, Mrs. Jackie. We both know this was going to happen someday.

No, no, no. Do I want to give her the same impression I gave LyRae on our first few encounters?

Maybe a bit more delicacy was needed?

As my mind struggled to find the best approach to this sort of thing, I resigned to just mentally beating myself up over and over for not being better prepared before calling her. Before I could hang up the phone, she answers. Oddly enough, she was actually taken by surprise to hear from me and wanted to know why I called her to begin with.

"Mrs. Jackie, I have a very important question to ask you."

"Yeah? Sure, what is it?" she asked.

"It is about LyRae," I said, allowing myself a short pause to recall the exact words I thought that might make my proposition more appealing.

"Ray, you are scaring me. What is it?" she replied, noticing the pause.

Picking up on the unwanted atmosphere I have unintentionally created for her, I just went straight to the point. "I want to ask her to marry me, and it would be an honor to have your blessing and support."

Silence. She did not say anything. If only I understood the context on how her breathing would better determine my chances at this conversation, my heart would not be waltzing around the walls of my chest at a 160 beats per minute. I wanted to fool myself that I partially expected this, and so I braved on with the conversation.

"I have been thinking about this for a very long time. I love your daughter, and I want to be with her for the rest of my life," I said while trying to mask my trembling voice. "I would like to ask for her hand in marriage."

She was always known to be very direct, but I also know the kind heart she carried with her.

I anxiously waited for her to respond.

It is the thing about waiting. You feel like you are turning into a kind of an instant massive receiver. An open box with absolutely nothing in it. I just sat there, letting my nervousness and blankness combined take over me.

I turned away from the wall for a moment and saw LyRae's framed face with mine. A photo of our first out-of-town trip together. On top of the table I studied at every night, sitting right next to piles of books and different mixes of crumpled paper. They were supposedly the building blocks of my hopes and dreams. The future success I was most certain I would achieve. In between the scatter was her face. Her warm and loving face.

Any feeling I may have lost on my leg from the nerve-racking wait, I started gaining back. From my little toes, rising up to my knees, all the way up to my heart. Though all this happened in just a split second, it felt much longer than that to me. That feeling of never-ending.

Then my heart skipped a beat, upon hearing the sound of a deep breath coming from the other end of the receiver, Mrs. Jackie. The sort of short pause a judge would do before the doling out the verdict.

"I do not want to make myself sound older than I am, but I will say this a thousand times if I have to—LyRae is my baby. I watched her grow up to become the woman she is now. I feel that my time raising her is almost over. No doubt that she still has more lessons to learn, but I will not be there to catch her whenever she feels the world has clipped her wings or to bring her back down to earth when her ego gets the best of her. She—" She wanted to continue, but something seems to have held her back. She took a quick breath and continued, "This is as much of you writing a chapter in your own life as it is with hers. Thank you for taking the time to tell me. I am happy that she found someone like you, and I would like to hear how you plan to propose."

This was the kind of wisdom LyRae always remembered fondly whenever we talked about her mother. I told her that it was of utmost importance that I obtain her permission first. I told her that I was not just securing LyRae's happiness but also letting her know that I could also be someone she could count on as family as early as now.

I then proceeded to tell her that even with all my eagerness to pop the question, I still had to wait for a perfect moment. She was very excited about it and even gave me a good tip on when to do it. (Do not worry, I will come back to this later). At the end of our conversation, she said, "I will give you my permission to marry my daughter." I was excited.

The next phone call I made was to LyRae's father, Timmy. I knew that it was going to be an easier conversation than the one I had with Mrs. Jackie—I guess I should be referring to her as Mom now. Timmy and I had become buddies. I thought back to the first time I met him. The first time you meet your girlfriend's father is always nerve-racking, and my experience was no different. I was nervous. This was the same person who suggested that LyRae ask her cousins to "meet" me. I did not make a big deal out of that, but I did not forget it either.

Will he like me?

Will he approve of me?

Would he ever let me drive his car?

These were the questions that ran through my mind when I met him.

"So, you are the young man who has been stalking my daughter in school," he said with a grave expression when I was introduced to him. I did not expect that opening. I was tongue-tied, and it took me a few moments to formulate a response. Before I could say anything, he broke into a smile. "Aw, come here you! I have heard so many good things about you." And he pulled me in for a hug.

"It is a pleasure to finally meet you, sir," I said.

"Please, call me Pop," he told me with a wave of his hand. "*Sir* makes me feel so old." And he smiled. He had one of those faces that you can trust. He had a big and easy smile. His hair was brown, and that smile, it reminded me of LyRae's own.

After spending some time with him, I learned that Timmy was a jokester. He never took anything too seriously. He was a carefree sort of person, and through the years, I had formed a good relationship with him.

The line stopped ringing. He finally answered.

"How you doing, Pop? I am calling to ask you a question," I said.

"Ray? Is this you?" he asked.

"Yes, it is me," I replied.

"What is your question?" he asked.

I took a deep breath and kind of just blurted out, "You know I love your daughter, and I want to spend the rest of my life with her, and I need to know if I can ask for her hand in marriage."

There was nothing but silence on the other line. Did I lose him?

"Hello? Pop? You still there?"

I heard him clear his throat. "Yes, I am still here," he replied. After a short pause, he asked, "Are you sure about this?"

I had never been surer of anything in my life. "Yes, I am positive," I said with a conviction and certainty that I hoped he could hear through the phone.

"Well, if you are sure, then I give you my blessing to marry my only child," he told me.

Relieved, I thanked him and put the receiver back in its cradle. I just needed to buy the perfect ring, and I was all set to propose.

I failed to fully grasp the gravity of perfect until I finally reach the shop. I spent a good amount of time ruminating on the possibilities with LyRae that I did not have time to consider the realities of actually choosing a ring. And not just any ring. The one ring that will rule over all my future joys. Ultimately, legitimize all my future children and substantiate all my future claims to love.

The weight of what is at stake bore down on me in every step I took. It was like hurling a gigantic third leg.

The choices made it all worse. There was just too many. I could not tell if one was perfect or was it the other. There was simply no way for me to survive the ordeal. So I called in the only reinforcement I needed. The one person who has always been there for me and LyRae. The person who can sum up our beginnings—Felicia.

Thanksgiving was coming up, and we planned to have Thanksgiving dinner at Mrs. Jackie's house with her family in South New Jersey. It was only two hours away by car, and we had a long weekend off from school, so we decided to drive. I dropped LyRae off first, as I had made plans to spend the day with my mother, who was in New Brunswick, New Jersey.

As I was approaching the familiar maroon-and-cream-colored apartment complex that is Schwartz-Roberson, I tried to imagine what my mother would say about me getting married and then I stopped myself, I already knew. I have two older sisters who are both thirteen and sixteen years my senior and two older brothers who were nineteen and twenty years my senior. My brother Orlander, who is nineteen years my senior, is deceased. I was my mother's youngest child, her baby. She would not take the news of my plans to propose very well.

I rang the bell, and it took her a few minutes to get to the door. While I was waiting I could hear her moving around from the outside.

"Just a minute!" she called from inside the apartment. "I will be right there!"

She was busy doing something. She opened the door.

"Ray!" she exclaimed. "You made it." She pulls me in for a big, long hug; and as she pulled away, she looked me up and down, saying, "I swear you keep getting taller each time I see you. Come inside, tell me what has been going on with you."

I stepped inside and looked around. She had not changed anything since the last time I came to see her. She led me to the kitchen, where we hold most of our conversations. I could see that she had been busy. It was a familiar scene—she always got like this around the holidays. She was cooking a few dishes for Thanksgiving dinner with her family. She had something in the oven, and it looked like she was doing the dishes at the same time before I came in. It never ceases to amaze me how she can cook and clean at the same time, not leaving a single mess. She started picking up where she left off in the sink, then checking the oven, tasting the sauce brewing up on the stove, all the while talking about her friends who were sick and stuck at home. I could not get a word in edgewise.

I realized I missed her as I watched her move about the kitchen. My mother, Elsie, is fifty-seven years old and does not look a day over forty. She was active and healthy, quite often mistaken as her daughters' older sister. I sat there, listened, and let her chat away.

"How is LyRae, by the way?" she asked suddenly.

"She is doing very well. We are having dinner at Mrs. Jackie's tonight—" I hesitated.

"Ray, what is it? I know you want to tell me something. Stop beating around the bush and just say it," she told me.

I could never hide anything from her.

"I am going to ask LyRae to marry me," I said.

Nothing can prepare a son from the shattering inside feeling only a question like this can bring.

She gave me that look, that half smirk and those narrowed eyes, all telling me that she is not happy. I know this look. I have seen it countless times before. She never takes any news of the women I date too well. As predicted, she was not pleased by my plans of proposing to LyRae.

As far as I can remember, I have always tried my best to stay on my mother's good side. It was a natural inkling to stay golden in her eyes. I did well in school. Made good impressions with my teachers and classmates. Offered to help with chores after doing my homework.

She felt threatened, as if this woman was going to steal her baby. I assured her that this was not going to happen. I stood up from where I was sitting at the kitchen table. I went to her, hugged her, and said, "Mother, I plan to marry her. She makes me very happy, and she adds so much to me. I hope you can trust and respect one of the biggest decisions I plan to make in my life."

She smiled, looked up at me, and said, "Are you sure about this decision?"

I looked at her, and without hesitation, I said, "With every fiber of my being, I am sure."

"Then there is no need to fret, my darling. I trust you. Though I cannot show it now as I have to deal with the ache in my heart for losing you over to someone. It is a motherly thing, you know. But I do trust you. I know I raised a good son. And making the decision to marry someone, being this sure, can only mean I raised someone who will only love and cherish the individual you will marry."

"I am sorry, Mother. I know this is selfish of me. But I see no other way."

"I know your father would be proud if he could understand." At this time my father was in a nursing home with dementia.

Even if I scoured the earth right then and there, turned it upside down, and did everything differently, I know nothing from this world could ever prepare me for that answer.

We said our good-byes. We said a lot of good-byes before arriving at the final one. I kissed her cheek like I always do and looked at her one last time before I turned to leave. She suddenly became older somehow. A bit deflated. We were just standing there, looking at each other for a brief moment. I opened the door, walked to my car, and got into my car. I adjusted the rearview mirror—she was still standing there. I drove away with this heavy lump stuck in my throat. There were no dry eyes in that parting.

I then proceeded to Mrs. Jackie's house, which was just an hour and a half away. I entered the house through the front door, which opened into the foyer. On my left side were steps that went upstairs, and to the right was the living room where I went through to get to the dining room. Again, it was Thanksgiving Day, November 23, 1989.

When I walked in, I saw that everybody was there for Thanksgiving dinner. There were between twenty to thirty people—her aunts and uncles, her cousins, everybody. The adults said their hellos, a little bit of chitchat here and there, while LyRae's brother and sister played in the next room with their cousins until dinner was ready.

We all gathered around the dinner table for the blessing, and Mrs. Jackie spoke. "Thank you, God, for this most amazing day, for my loving family, for keeping them safe as they made their way here, for the glorious food laid out before us, amen."

"Amen!" everyone said.

"Before we dig in," Mrs. Jackie continued, "Ray wants to say something." And with a knowing look, she nodded in my direction.

At this point, I was already very nervous. It was one thing to plan it and another to see it through. All day, I kept running situations in my head where anything could go wrong, and now that the moment was here, I did not know what to think. I just knew that I wanted to do this. I waited two months for a perfect moment to ask her, and here it was, mine for the taking.

LyRae was standing next to me; and I turned to her, took her hands in mine, and looked her in the eyes. And then for everybody to hear, I said, "I have been extremely happy. You make my life worth living, and because of that"—I reached into my pocket for the ring and got down on one knee while LyRae started crying—"will you marry me?" In between tears, she said yes.

Everyone cheered for us and said their congratulations, and we all had a scrumptious meal.

Mrs. Jackie had outdone herself that evening.

I am used to large family gatherings and eating, but Mrs. Jackie quite simply takes the cake. Serving dish after dish that looked to me like it could feed the entire clan for an entire week. I saw then where LyRae got her propensity for large-sized servings.

I also realized that I had been hungry the whole time. All day long it felt like I was running around town like a chicken with my head cut off. I have done a lot as a young man, but this proposing-to-the-love-of-your-life business was not something I imagine doing more than once. At least, in my mind, I thought it at that time.

The plump roasted turkey was the star of the show. I could not stop stuffing my face with it, coupled with a puddle of steaming gravy and mashed potatoes. When I saw the desserts, I went all out.

After dinner, we left Mrs. Jackie's house to drive to Pop's to tell him the good news. He and Mrs. Jackie had divorced a long time ago, and he was having Thanksgiving dinner with his family at LyRae's great-grandmother's house, where holidays with the family are usually spent.

Pop's family was even a larger one, so I was not surprised to see about forty people there for Thanksgiving. I spent a lot of time with them over the years, and I was already familiar and comfortable with most of them.

We literally burst through the door and announced, "We got engaged!"

Everyone fell quiet and looked at us blankly, until Timmy broke the silence when he said, "Now, Ray, you are going to have to propose to her here too."

The rest of the family nodded in agreement.

I got down on one knee and proposed again.

LyRae cried again.

"Why are you crying again?" I asked her.

"I do not know!" she exclaimed while wiping tears from her face, and we all laughed.

CHAPTER 2

RENEWAL OF VOWS

Mr. Thompson.

"*M*r. Thompson, are you feeling okay?"

I open my eyes and think for a moment that maybe I am still in my dreams.

The nurse calls me again.

"Mr. Thompson?"

No, this is the continuity of reality. This is where I am now.

It is not like in the movies after all.

In there, all you need to do is to see. Here, everything comes to me like one quick jab after another.

It is way too bright. I must have let my memories take over me for longer than it seemed. I must have looked like I was struggling or laughing like I did when I recalled LyRae crying during my second proposal. I squint at the person who is talking to me, and I see a nurse standing over me. She is not the same one from before.

"I just remembered something funny," I tell her.

"The doctor will be here any moment. Do you need anything?"

"No, I am all right," I reply.

She is young and maybe even new. She is checking something on the laptop in the corner of my room. She takes my vitals and encodes it.

"All right then." She leaves and closes the door behind her.

The doctor is coming soon. I want to close my eyes and rest. I want to continue and think about all my greatest hits. Those memories always make me feel good. I take a deep breath and let my memories take over me once again.

Like any other morning for the past twenty-five years, I woke up beside my wife, LyRae. I prepared my clothes for the day, and as usual, after fighting the urges to go back to sleep, I got up. I walked to the sink in the bathroom and looked at myself in the ;mirror.

Can you imagine? It has been twenty-five years, I thought.

I laid out my all-white suit. It was something I had bought for this occasion. I had decided to wear a silver undershirt and a silver fedora hat. I admired it for a minute before packing it up neatly and waited for LyRae to get ready to go.

We drove about an hour and a half to Silver Spring Marriott in Silver Spring, Maryland to check in, just listening to the radio and singing along from time to time. Back when we lived in Baltimore, we had joined a church and it was our former pastor from that church did we call and make arrangements with to renew our vows for this day.

We drove twenty minutes from the hotel to Washington, D. C., and as we pulled up to Howard University, I see the familiar red-brick buildings I frequented so much for four years of my young adult life. I stepped out of the car. It was a typical hot day in July. I had almost forgotten how warm it was in D. C.

It was July 23, 2016, and I was back at Howard University to celebrate the love that I found and started here, the love that made my life what it is, the love that made me the man I am today. A husband and a father of two amazing children.

We parked behind the Fine Arts building and walked toward the Blackburn Center, where our second wedding was to be held. I looked around me and realized not too much had changed. A wave of nostalgia stopped me dead in my tracks. Bison pride streamers still hung from the windows, the same white blinds still shaded the rooms from the harsh rays of the sun, and the bison pictures and memorabilia were arranged out front.

I looked at my wife and said, "LyRae, I used to walk this way every time I came to see you back then."

"I know, honey." She tugged on my arm and pulled me in for a quick kiss on the cheek.

I was excited and extremely thankful that this ceremony was made possible; and to celebrate it here, where it all started, was an amazing blessing.

We entered the Blackburn Center; made our way to the second-floor terrace, the Hilltop Terrace; and from there you could see the McMillan Reservoir and the tops of the trees that surrounded it. It was a lovely day for an outdoor wedding. The terrace was filled with 120 seats, divided into two sections. In the middle was an aisle for the participants of the wedding to walk through.

Our guests started to arrive, slowly trickling in, and next thing I knew, people started to fill the rows of seats that were prepared for them. We invited a 120 guests, and among them, seated in front, were Mom and Pop, LyRae's grandmother, as well as my mother. They had all driven from New Jersey for this, and I was so happy to see that they made it.

I started noticing the differences between this day and our wedding day a quarter century ago. For one thing, I was not nearly as nervous as I was at our first wedding. This day was an affirmation of the decision we made back then, only proving to each other that we would keep our promise to love each other till death do us part. I straightened my suit jacket and walked unto the terrace to take my turn to walk down the aisle.

I looked to my left, and I saw my son, RJ. He was all grown-up. Where did all that time go? He was twenty-three years old, and maybe, someday soon, he will be where I was standing. I let my mind drift to how I would react if he ever tells me that he wants to marry the love of his life, a conversation I never got to have with my own father.

Around the time of our first wedding, my father was in a nursing home where I visited often. Some days he recognized me, and others, I was a complete stranger. He had Alzheimer's disease, and it was hard to reason with him. I went to visit him hoping to be able to tell him about that milestone in my life, on good days he was lucid and he remembers everything. He would call me Ray like he did when I was growing up and ask me about school. The day I came to visit to deliver the news of my engagement was not a particularly good one. I could tell from the way he was gazing out the window that he hardly recognized me or the place he was in. He could not, even if he tried.

"Dad, LyRae and I are getting married," I said.

He looked at me like I was a stranger. "Well, congratulations, mister. Who is the lucky lady?" he politely replied.

My heart sank as I realized that he could not share my joy. I remember leaving the nursing home that day downhearted.

So I imagined if RJ introduced his future wife. I would be extremely happy for him and hope that I showed him enough love, love for his sister and his mother to set a good example for him and his future family, and I want to remember it. He was standing with me as my best man. He is the best man in every sense of the term. Like a cool breeze on a hot summer day, he dances through life—a very laid-back kind of guy. He is always liked working in the background, with a very quiet and mild-mannered personality.

I looked down the aisle; and my daughter, Son'Serae, was making her way toward us, all smiles, as the maid of honor. She was twenty years old; and she is the strongest, most outspoken person I have ever met, always the leader of the group, and the complete opposite of her brother. I remember when she was little, she would pick on other children just to hear them cry.

"But it was funny, Daddy," she used to say.

I smiled at the memory and at my baby girl who was wearing a white off-the-shoulder formal dress that she picked out with her mother, accented by her signature white flowers and rose-gold jewelry.

LyRae took her turn to walk down the aisle and to the altar to take her place by my side. Everyone stood up to look at her as she made her way to me. LyRae, my wife of twenty-five years, the mother of my children, my everything, my angel. She walked down the aisle in a simple white wedding dress with cap sleeves, where the front hem falls just below the knees and the back falls to her ankles, creating a playful yet formal finish.

She was a sight to behold as always. I will never think of her as less than royalty come to grace the room with her presence. I think of the last twenty-five years of our lives, and I do not regret a single thing. I would do it all over again in a second as long as she was by my side. My heart was so full of love for her.

When she reached us, our former pastor began the ceremony with a prayer and a scripture. We then took turns to read our vows.

LyRae reconfirmed her love to me.

"Thank you, God! Oh how I love you for blessing me.
You gave me a husband who loves me unconditionally.
You gave me a husband who prays for me.
You gave me a husband who puts me before himself.
You gave me a husband who puts me before everyone but you.
You gave me a husband who worries about me.
You gave me a husband who takes care of me.
You gave me a husband who provides for me.
You gave me a husband who believes in doing things together.
You gave me a husband who takes the time to listen, even
when I am not saying anything.
You gave me a husband who encourages me to follow my dreams.
You gave me husband who allowed me to put our children first.
You gave me a husband who loves our children.
You gave me a husband who cares about our children.
You gave me a husband that provides for our children.
You gave me a husband who I do not have to fight with about
our children.
You gave me a husband that I could not have picked myself.
Father, I thank you."

As I was about to read mine, I had to pause for a second and look at my copy again. I tried to focus because the words looked like they were moving around on the page I wrote them on. The letters looked like swirls that were jumbled together, and they started to float in different directions.

"It was on 6 July 1991, you gave me your hand and we were pronounced husband and wife. This was one of the greatest days of my life. As we planned ahead for our life together, I am not certain if either of us ever could have imagined twenty-five years later.

It was over these past twenty-five years we have lived in Silver Spring;

Maryland; Fairfax; Virginia; Owings Mills; Maryland; and now York, Pennsylvania. The Lord has allowed for us to purchase two homes and a number of vehicles. However, most of all, the Lord blessed us with the birth of our two children—Ray Edwards Thompson Jr. on October 8, 1992, and Son'Serae Auntwanette Thompson on May 15, 1996. Both of these lives given to us have been two of the greatest highlights of our marriage and these past twenty-five years."

I started to feel light-headed, but I pushed on.

"As I survey the last twenty-five years with you, I can honestly say that I would not have traded anything for the time we have spent together. You are my life. You are one of the greatest joys of life, and for that, I say thank you. Thank you for being there for me every step of the way. Thank you for being the most incredible wife that any man could ever imagine or dream of.

*Thank you for being the mother of my two children; you have been there for them both. Thank you for being my wife, my confidant, my lover, and my all in all. Sitting back and reflecting, to I realize that my soul is that special place **where** only God and you dwell As I rededicate my life to you for the next twenty-five plus years, I look forward to all that God will do with us and for us. Just know my heart belongs to you . . ."*

After I read my vows, I had to ask RJ to find me a chair to sit down on. He got me a chair and some water to drink. The light-headedness passed, and I felt all right again. I told myself that I just forgot to eat because of all the excitement of the day. In case standing up would cause another wave of light-headedness, I remained seated for the rest of the ceremony.

At the end of the ceremony, I looked at my wife and whispered, "Twenty-five years and here we are."

She smiled and said, "Here we are." She kissed me. Our guests stood up and gave us a round of applause.

Our guests were then led to the hilltop lounge and were served hors d'oeuvres while we, the wedding party, had our pictures taken by a professional photographer who was covering the whole event. He is also my cousin, Walter. I helped myself to hors d'oeuvres, I realized I had not eaten yet. I immediately felt better. That was all I needed to do. How could I forget to eat?

LyRae and I led RJ and Son'Serae to the Yard, along with my cousin, the photographer who took our pictures out on the terrace and the campus.

The Fine Arts building was close enough, so we showed them the exact location where I saw their mother for the first time, where our epic love story started. I wonder sometimes if they ever get tired of listening to me tell that story, but I will never get tired of telling it. We were off getting our pictures taken for about thirty minutes and proceeded back to the Hilltop Lounge.

When we were ready, we then made our way to the reception in the banquet hall to join our guests who were led there after the hors d'oeuvres. We had reserved half of the ballroom. The DJ introduced the wedding party. RJ and Son'Serae were introduced to our guests as they entered the banquet hall and took their seats, and then we were introduced next. The reception proceeded without a hitch. Everyone was seated at their table of choice, and the program started as planned.

After we were introduced and made our entrance, it was time for our first dance. LyRae and I were at the center of the room as our smiling guests looked on. There was an awkward little pause before the music started where we just giggled like high school sweethearts. To fill the awkward silence, I bowed in her direction. She laughed again and curtsied. The music began, and our eyes locked. I took her hand in mine, wrapped my arm around her, and pulled her close. We let the music guide us as we danced to Lalah Hathaway's "Angel." It was not a song that reminded me of a specific period in my life or a specific moment, but it so perfectly encapsulated my feelings for LyRae that I chose it to be the song for this dance. From that moment forward, that song would remind me of this exact moment in my life.

> *Dreams are dreams, some dreams come true*
> *I found a real dream, baby, when I found you*
> *You are so strong, but tender too*
> *Love like ours is heaven sent*
> *Each a day to remember*
>
> *I feel so safe, so secure with you*
> *You give me love, you keep right on giving*
> *Fill me up baby, with the joy of living*
> *When things get tough I can always turn to you.*

25

When the song finished, I escorted LyRae to our seats. We were seated in front of all our guests, where we could see everyone and everyone could see us. We then proceeded with dinner, catered by Howard University's caterers, Sodexo. All the guests were called per table to proceed to the buffet area and help themselves to the food that was prepared.

My daughter, Son'Serae, stood up after a while, got everyone's attention and gave her toast:

> *"To my parents,*
>
> *I want to congratulate you on your twenty-five years of blissful marriage.*
> *In my lifetime I have never seen you fight. The two of you have always showed me what a marriage should look like, and I definitely look forward to getting married because I know what to expect out of my spouse and I know how I should carry myself.*
> *I just want to congratulate you all again, and I definitely look forward to seeing what is in store for you in the next twenty-five years."*

Everyone cheered, and I thought, *I am so blessed.*

RJ took his turn to give his best man speech:

> *"Thank you for showing me and Son'Serae how to treat our significant other.*
> *Y'all have showed us that communication is key to making a relationship work for twenty-five years. Even though someone was not always the best at it. Thank you for showing us what a marriage is supposed to look like."*

I was touched by my children's words. I did not realize how proud they were of us. I was not always a perfect father, but I tried my best to provide for them, take care of them, take care of their mother. LyRae was sitting quietly next to me, tears of joy falling down her beautiful face.

It was time for the cake cutting. We stood up and walked down from the platform and walked around to the front of the platform where the cake was waiting for us. It was an interesting one, a three-layered cake with our family photos all around it. I took the knife—not the server, as advised by our baker—and cut a small piece from the bottom tier, more advice from our dear baker. We proceeded to feed each other bite-size pieces of the cake and let the rest of the program run its course.

After this, we went around the ballroom with our children to meet and talk to our guests. We had our pictures taken at each table. That part of the program took up the bulk of the reception. We then proceeded to the center of the room and gave our speech as a couple, where we thanked everyone for coming.

After a small photo op with our remaining guests, we went back to the hotel in Maryland. We ran into a few people there, but we did not get together with anyone until breakfast the next day. Two of our friends, Christopher (my best friend) and Gale, who came to the wedding from Atlanta treated us. There is an interesting backstory to how I met Christopher, but we will get to that later. We walked down the street and into a chic little place with brick walls and wooden furniture with chalkboards placed strategically around the area with cute quotes and tips for your food that made the place homey. We all sat and placed our orders that were served with surprising speed. "So, Dad," RJ said in between bites of bacon and eggs, "what do you think the next twenty-five years will be like?"

I took a sip of my water, looked at RJ, and said, "I hope to attend your wedding soon."

He grinned and took a large sip of his orange juice.

At that time, RJ was single, so everyone laughed.

"I want to hold my grandbabies," I said as RJ pretended to choke on his orange juice.

LyRae interrupted, "I like where you are going with this, but Son'Serae needs to finish school and RJ needs to get settled first."

"Of course! We are talking twenty-five years, honey," I said.

It is different when I hear myself say it out loud. It sounds unreal. Like I am listening to someone saying something that happened to somebody else.

Has it really been that long?

I cannot say enough about how good the children have been. When

LyRae told me she was pregnant, it felt like something that had been stuck with me for a very long time was suddenly plucked out. Like wax on very hairy legs.

I am going to be a father.

Being a husband was not a terrifying idea. It was a decision I made because of LyRae. A conscious and deliberate decision that has thickened and grown roots over the years that I have spent with her. But being a father is not. I am supposed to know right away even if I have never met the child. I have no idea what kind of person he or she is, and I am supposed to be responsible for that: the end product. What kind of decision could I possibly start with when I have nothing to work on?

It took some time for me to recover from the thought.

Will I ever do this right?

How do I know I am doing it right?

My relationship with my own father was perfect to make a man out of me. To me, it was enough to prepare me for being a husband and a father. At least, that is what I always thought. He showed me a lot of the things I did not want to be and things that did not want to happen to me. My father was the kind of person who would take the shirt off his back and offer it to you if you needed it. Many people took advantage of that, and I never wanted that to happen to me. My father was a reverend and an assistant pastor.

I think about my children, and they have no clue how much I struggled in the beginning.

"Did we lose you somewhere, honey? Looks like you have gone off somewhere. What is on your mind?" said LyRae.

"Sorry, just, you know, seeing how good-looking our children turned out to be," I replied.

"Dad, cut it out. Save the make-your-children-squirm-because-I-can exercise for home," RJ said, half chuckling and half blushing.

"Glad they take after you, hon. Otherwise, I would not know what to do with them. Probably give them away or something." I laughed.

"They take as much from me as they do from you. But you already know that." LyRae smiled knowingly.

Chris and Gale chuckled.

"You two are the best!" Gale said. "And you have to get me in touch with your caterer! The food was amazing yesterday! I liked how there was so much to choose from, and the petit fours were splendid!"

"You know what was interesting to me was the seating, how the wedding party was placed in the middle on a raised platform. They looked like royalty, didn't they? And, Gale, did you notice how everyone was seated at round tables and Ray and his family were seated at a long table? It was such a sight!" Christopher interjected.

"Yes, it was, and the wedding cake, wow!" Gale said. "It was delicious! What happened to the rest of it? I saw there was a lot left after the reception."

"You know what, I have no idea. LyRae?" I asked my wife.

"We gave most of it away. I think Earl and Joyce took some home. We can stop by on the way to Pennsylvania if you'd like," LyRae told me.

"Let us do that!" I said.

We finished up breakfast and walked back to the hotel to check out. We said our good-byes and stopped by Earl and Joyce's place for some cake. We then started making our way back home to York, Pennsylvania.

"Welcome Home."

We have had the same planked quote since we moved in. It is a reminder. Like a switch on and off in my head. Whatever troubles I may have at work or anywhere else, when I see home, I try not to bring them in and leave them outside the door. It is the same with everything that I do. The way I set my alarm and wake up at the same time every morning. It is part of my daily performance. I am a baton twirler of my own private marching band. I find comfort in its humdrum.

Everything looks the same. Except it is not. Being on the road for long must have recalibrated my brain. I seem to be seeing things differently even when they are not at all that different. Home is as typical as any family home can be: five bedrooms, a living room, a dining room, and a family room.

The home I grew up in was much smaller. Not just the number of people in it but more on its sense of purpose, propagating, vibrating within its walls. Before his illness took over, my father was an assistant pastor. He was the kind of person that had a larger than life gait about him. He walked among his congregation as a giant. He was their David. Everyone turned to him for strength, for guidance, for help. They would climb up his shoulders, and he would willingly take the shirt off his back if he needed to. He lived the kind of life a modern-day saint would choose.

I was in every way amazed by him. But what he had done, what he made out of himself, also set the bar too high for me to reach. Having the front row seat to all his selflessness and dedication to do good was not at all easy. Even trying to do good, like everything else, comes with a price.

I saw my dad constantly being taken advantage of. People came to him for money that most of them never returned. People came to him for advice that most of them threw back at him or twisted around, never taking it to heart. People just kept coming and coming at him, taking everything from him, without a single thought on giving back. I guess you can say that I saw the good together with the bad. And I promised myself never to allow people to treat me the way they did my father.

Like all sons of great men, I was one of those who did not wish to succumb to his magnitude, to the enormity of his work: constantly improving the lives of others through deeds and God's words. I did not want to be a mere afterthought of his accomplishments. To be his son, his only son. I did not want to be small.

So I tried to be better. And by being better, I did what I could to avoid following his footsteps.

All those years of just observing my dad, I knew how to run a ministry like I knew the back of my hand. It was something that I knew how to do before I learned anything else. It is one of the perks of growing up in one. The inner workings of how to run a place like that flows through my blood.

At thirteen, I realized that I was bound to do God's work. To live my life in the service of Him.

But I did not accept this in the beginning. I tried to find my own path by deviating from the one set before me. I did not take the pastoral courses. I did not play by the rules. I played out my tiny well-thought-out rebellions for as long as I could. I avoided coming to terms with what I knew I was supposed to do. I was in denial.

I did what any teenager would do when overwhelmed with responsibilities: I left. I ran away from home, running away from God. I left the church and community I grew up in and moved to Washington, D. C. I did not heed what God was asking me to do.

For a long time, I was just going through the motion of living in a new city: adjusting to its rhythm, making new friends, and going to classes at Howard University, but not really knowing where I am going.

Until I found a church. It was the first church LyRae and I joined as a couple, the New Bethel Church of God in Christ (COGIC). We were just visitors for the first four years until we joined them in 1990. Our son, RJ, and daughter, Son'Serae, were both dedicated there.

By 1995 we were already living in Baltimore, and it was too much to drive back and forth to D. C. to go to church, so we had to leave New Bethel and start looking for a church in Baltimore. We went to several different churches until we found The Good Shepherd COGIC in the middle of 1997. We did not join the church right away because RJ had gone to New Jersey for three weeks. It was not until the end of August of that year, after RJ returned home, that we joined the church.

This church was just like the one I had at home in New Jersey. I met the pastor who ran it. He was just like my dad in many ways. The father I left and refused to become.

With him, I can be myself. I did not feel pressured to be someone else. To be this great son that I was expected to be back home.

I was more relaxed. And I enjoyed doing the things that I never enjoyed doing before in my old church. Back at the old church where I grew up, it always felt like someone was watching me. Lurking behind me and judging me at the same time. I was looked upon as a reflection of my father, so I was supposed to act in a certain way and conduct myself in a manner that was appropriate for a pastor's son. But in this new church, there was none of that. I did not have to second guess my every action. I did not have to please people. I can be just me.

And because of that, I learned to be more confident about myself. I sensed a new strength in me that can only be built from the wreckage of a released burden.

But there was still something missing. The time I spent with the pastor helped me see what was in front of me, showed me the person that I was at that time. He bared all my flaws and all my fears.

What was not clear then was the person that I can be. The person that I was meant to become.

The future awaits, and I was unsure.

Around that time, I was already doing a good amount of work at the church. LyRae was a Sunday school teacher, a teacher for Vacation Bible School, as well as she started the nursery in that church. I was also the chairman of the men's department. All the men of the church would get together on a monthly basis to talk about issues related to men, anything that they were going through, like health issues or anything along those lines. I was also the lead armor bearer. I was responsible for taking care of the pastor and all his needs. I was his go-to person.

I was fulfilling my duties; but my other father, my mentor and pastor, could see through my uncertainty. I felt I needed to do something more, and I told him so. He sent me off on a journey hoping that I would find what it was that I truly wanted from this life. He told me that he can only go as far as helping me with the now. But as for tomorrow, what my future self holds, I would have to discover that for myself. It is a decision I would have to make on my own. In order for me to move forward to the right direction, I needed to spend some time alone to understand what I am destined for.

The timing of that journey was everything. If I had taken it before I got to know the pastor, if I had gone on with it without the renewed sense of self I have discovered along the way, if I had headed back home instead of heeding my pastor's advice, it would have gone all to waste.

There are simply lessons that we are not ready for at certain phases in our lives. We never truly understand until it shines a light on a pain point.

I learned to read the Bible with more attentive thought. I have read it more times than an average person would in one lifetime. In all my years of rereading and revisiting it, I have never read a scripture that hit home as much as the book of John, the book my pastor asked me to read, my journey.

You have to understand that I was at the lowest point of my life then. I was confused. I was happy with where I was. But there was this nagging feeling inside me. A voice in my head saying I was not doing enough. I was where I belonged. I felt at home in my new church. I found my rock in my pastor. But I was not moving. I was not growing. Everyone around me had one or two things going on which they found meaning in doing. I, on the other hand, had none. I was doing more than anyone at the church, but not a single one of them gave meaning to me.

When I read John again, the first few verses stuck. I have read it a thousand times before, even listened to it a few times during Sunday service. But experiencing it once again at a time when I was most troubled—it made all the difference.

It is true what they say about the basic instinct of man to fear the unknown. The effect quadruples when you come to terms with something that you've known for some time but refuse to acknowledge.

In chapter 5 of the book of John (verses 1–9), it talks about a man who was an invalid. Jesus asked him if he wanted to be made whole, and the man just gave him excuses. That is when it hit me, that during all these years, my running away from God, I was simply giving Him so many excuses why I could not do what was asked of me. What God asked of me was to become an oracle of Him and to preach the gospel. I knew this, but I kept giving excuses why I could not do that. I would say I am too tall for this, I will be seen as a freak of nature; I am too outspoken; my dress code is all wrong; my taste is too flashy.

When Jesus made the impotent man rise and said, "Take up thy bed and walk," he made him whole again. That state of being whole, of being complete again, is what I have been longing for all along. I did not know what I was missing. His wisdom seeped through me like cold water would to lips exposed long under the desert sun. Tears of realization ran down my face as I read them again. The answer was right there. It took me a long time to get here, but the timing could not be more right. I knew what I had to do. My voice trembled as I pounded my fist on my chest for the words to come out. They had been hovering in there for so long, just waiting to be said. To be found again. I listened to the old beat of my heart and let it out:

I am going to be a pastor.

As I went back to my pastor, the words kept ringing in my head. I have delayed it for far too long. I had to leave my home and find a new home just to arrive at my real purpose. *I knew that becoming a pastor was the end goal; however, I had to become a minister first. So I did.*

After becoming a minister and working in the church diligently, I began to feel an unrest. It could not wait any longer. I had to start immediately, but I felt that it was not going to happen in Baltimore. I had done everything I needed to do there. It was time to go. When I shared this with my pastor, he was upset and did not want me to leave but I knew

I had reached a point where I could not grow anymore. I then left The Good Shepherd Church of God In Christ and moved my membership to a church in York, Pennsylvania, in October 2006. The church me and my family joined was called Maranatha Church of God in Christ (COGIC).

Over time, LyRae became the church secretary, the secretary of the board of directors, as well as the armor bearer to the pastor. The pastor of the church was female, and it made sense for LyRae to be armor bearer. I became somewhat of an assistant pastor, but that was not my title. My title was church administrator. I handled the business aspects of the church, such as paying bills, meeting with auxiliaries, making sure that everything was running smoothly. All the financial responsibilities were my responsibility. It was a very good training ground for me. I was able to truly understand the workings of being a pastor of a church. The only responsibility I did not have was preaching to the congregation every Sunday. I did preach from time to time, maybe once a month on a Sunday, simply because my pastor asked me to.

One day, she asked me, "Why are you not ordained, Ray?"

"My former pastor and I never made it that far," I said.

"We have to get your ordained," she said, leaving no room for argument.

This conversation happened in November of 2006. Typically, becoming ordained happens in the month of August. So we put together a plan going forward. I enrolled in Bible sessions, which required me to take various classes to become ordained, as they were a requirement.

I began my training to become an ordained elder in the Churches of God in Christ. Most people referred to me as a minister, but sometimes individuals would mistake me for an elder. My teachers were so impressed by my dedication and comprehensive knowledge of the scriptures. The scriptures became almost second nature to me because of all the work I had done working very closely with my dad while growing up, along with all of the time spent with my former pastor.

At some point I was told not to participate in a few classes as I already know most of them by heart. One of the professors had asked me why I was taking these classes that I seem to already know the material. I had a conversation with the dean and stopped taking the classes. I was a special case.

I found that people were drawn to my sermons. Preaching the word of

God became my sort of specialty, my hook. It was easy for me to connect with people that way. And the congregation as a whole were very kind and generous. I experienced less amount of difficulty during my transition to more mature roles in the church. I was invited to carry out pastoral duties among groups on several occasions. I also had opportunities to offer counsel and reconcile troubled families.

At the back of my mind, I was also trying to be careful not to cross any lines. Not to fall for the same trap doors as my father did. Genuine kindness comes from a special place. And it being special, people tend to seek it out and find ways to trample on it. I learned everything I could from my dad's experiences. I made it a point to set boundaries with the people I try to help. I removed myself from compromising situations as much as I could. The kind of situation where I knew by instinct, nothing good would come out of. Anything that is related to legal matters, I steered clear of that in every way I can. I focused on the work at hand.

The year went by so fast. I did not realize how fast until I was ordained as an elder sometime in August of 2007. I stayed on at Maranatha for another two years. In 2009 I started a new church where I was the pastor, Temple Global Ministries COGIC. A year later, I moved the church out of COGIC because the reformation was no longer conducive for the size of the church. Therefore, I decided to become a nondenominational church.

CHAPTER 3

THE BIG MOVE

*B*linding light.

As I open my eyes, I see nothing but light and white.

Am I alive?

Did Hollywood get it right?

Is this what happens when you meet your Maker?

No. As my vision adjusts, I see white-paneled ceilings, white paneled-walls. I am in a big, roomy unit in a hospital.

Oh, that is right. I am in a hospital.

I look around at my surroundings, trying to process it. I look down at myself. White sheets cover my body. I look to my side, and I see I am attached to an IV line and beeping monitors tracking my vitals.

"Is anyone there?" I call out.

My lips move, but the sound that comes out are barely even words.

I try again. "Is anyone there?" It is only just a whisper.

My wife appears at my bedside. "I am right here. What do you need?"

I do not need anything. I only need to see her.

As I lie here awake, I try to recall the events that got me here. In a rush, all the memories start flooding my mind. Fast-forwarded events bombarding, flooding, causing my head to hurt. Memories come to the surface all at once, and it is too much.

Loss of movement and normal bodily functions.

Different smiling faces, poking and prodding.

Liver failing.

Bladder failing.

Blood pressure crashing.

Kidneys failing.

It is all too much.

I do not know how I start to drift away again, but I just do.

I find myself once more hidden in my thoughts, hidden in my memories.

As the sound of the slow, steady beeping of my monitors fade into the background, everything around me slowly disappears and in its place is a new, yet familiar, scenario.

The sound of fast-turning wheels on pavement fill my eardrums.

The hospital walls fade away and turn into open air around me.

The doctors and nurses vanish.

My wife LyRae is next to me in the passenger's seat.

Trees, with their leaves slowly falling, take over.

It is a blur of greens and blues.

In front of me is a long, winding road, waiting, inviting.

I am suddenly in a different time, a different place.

I was taking exit 177 on I-85, and in a few moments I found myself on N Roxboro St, headed to Durham, North Carolina. LyRae, RJ, and I were on our way to see Son'Serae, who had fallen ill. I was worried about her and felt that we needed to check up on her. Son'Serae, at the time, was staying at the dorms on North Carolina Central University's campus.

After driving through seemingly endless lines of pavement, entering this part of North Carolina was refreshing. We drove through roads lush with tall trees on each side, and in some short stretches, the trees would form a canopy above us. It was beautiful. I caught a glimpse of Duke Park to my right, where the entire Duke neighborhood coined its name from, and if memory serves, this was one of the oldest neighborhoods in the area, dating back to the 1920s. We drove by houses that maintained its Colonial Revival style: two-story houses with brick veneers and a combination of neoclassical components that gave the entire neighborhood a quaint and picturesque quality.

We turned left on E Lawson St to see Son'Serae at the university, and as we arrived, I recall the time LyRae told me about move-in day when she drove with Son'Serae here. She told me that the dorm room was a mess of her things strewn about untidily in desperate need of organizing. But when I saw it, I was not surprised to see the mess that was typical of my daughter. She was always excited to see us, but whenever she was feeling ill, she was always more mellow and really not herself.

My daughter has always had a strong character. She was always independent, and seeing a frail and sickly side of her worried me.

She was used to a certain kind of cooking when she lived with us. Everything LyRae cooked was baked. Ever since Son'Serae moved away to college, she was on a meal plan and she had a hard time adjusting to the food. They were more or less the same food as she had at home, but these were more fried and laden with oil. She was in and out of the hospital, and she was sick a lot. We drove to North Carolina to see her as much as we could during the first two years of her college life.

"Hello, my baby girl, how are you?" I said as she gave me and her mother a hug.

"Hi, Mommy. Hi, Daddy! I have been better. I had to stay in the hospital because of dehydration. They would not let me out until I urinated! It was horrible. I could not stop throwing up before that, but I am so happy to see you," she said enthusiastically.

"What did you eat this time?" LyRae asked.

"I think it was the spices in the cafeteria food that I had or from dinner when my girls and I went out for dinner the other night. I am not sure. Oh, we went out. We were celebrating a successful project."

She does this sometimes, hop from one thought to another.

"Aw, baby girl, you know how sensitive your stomach is. You should be more careful about what you eat. You have to learn to cook your own food," LyRae advised.

"What was your project about?" I asked.

"It is exciting actually. My professor really enjoyed our presentation of a social media marketing plan for this new restaurant called Enrique's. They serve Spanish food."

"How does that work?" LyRae asked.

"Well, we basically set up their social media profiles, and after doing an intensive market study, we have a specific target market for the ads wherein they only pop up on this specific market's news feed."

"That is great, baby girl! We are so proud of you."

We spent the next couple of hours doing a tour of the university and stopped by a Walmart before checking into a hotel so that LyRae can shop for a few things she thought Son'Serae was missing and make sandwiches for her as well.

We walked down the aisles of Walmart. I was pushing the cart and watching my favorite girls enjoy each other's company, and I thought, *Thank God for them.* My life is so much more meaningful because of them. I cannot imagine a different life.

After dropping Son'Serae off back at the university, we made our way to the Marriott Residence Inn at Brier Creek in Raleigh. It was only thirty minutes away from Durham. We found this gem of a hotel during one of our previous trips, and as we entered the lobby, we saw the familiar staff, who greeted us cheerfully.

"How are you today, Mr. and Mrs. Thompson? We are very happy to see you again," the hotel front desk receptionist said.

"We are happy to be back in North Carolina," I told her.

Whenever I look at the front desk, I always think that it was a place for business but then most of their guests are frequent fliers, being that it was so close to the airport and people usually only stay for meetings or to catch a late flight. It had a very corporate feel to it, but I felt it was a second home. The hotel staff contribute a lot to that feeling. I gave my card to Sheila, the front desk receptionist; and as she took it, "It is been a while since you've been here," she observed.

I smiled. "Yes, but we are back! We are thinking about moving here," I told her as she swiped my card and handed over our room key. We had a long day, so we decided to stay in and order room service. We had to drive to Charlotte the following morning.

"That is great! North Carolina is a lovely place to live."

At breakfast the next day, we encountered Hannah, as we always do, when we go to breakfast at this hotel.

"Hello there!" she greeted us cheerfully as she saw us enter the breakfast area.

"Good morning, Hannah, it is very nice to see you again," LyRae said to her.

"You seem to be missing at least two people in your group," she noted, observing that RJ and Son'Serae were not around when they usually are every time we come here.

"Oh, you will see them again for sure. They should be around tomorrow," I told her. "How's your mother?"

"Still in physical therapy, but she is doing much better now. She is able to walk and talk properly now, which is a very good sign. She is recovering quite well. Are you guys going to stay here long this time?"

"We are staying a few days, but we are actually driving to Charlotte tomorrow."

"Are you going to catch the Taste of Charlotte?" she asked.

"Yes, indeed we are! We are very excited about it actually," I responded.

"Try the burgers at Brownstone's sandwich shop, they are my favorite!"

"We will definitely do that! Thanks for the recommendation!"

We then started getting our food from the buffet.

Hannah asked, "Did you get enough at the buffet, and was it good?"

"Thank you, Hannah, the food was terrific and you have a good day," I replied.

LyRae and I ate our breakfast in comfortable silence, each of us reading the paper. We drove to Charlotte shortly after that.

Ah, the city of Charlotte.

We are happy to be back in North We had always had it in our minds to maybe move there. We heard so many good things about the place. It has an interesting history. Charlotte was actually named after Queen Charlotte of England, but shortly after, it was supposedly the first city to declare its independence from Great Britain after the battle of Lexington in 1775, and if this is true, it would have preceded the US Declaration of Independence by a year or more.

It is now the biggest city in North Carolina, the home of the Bobcats (now the Charlotte Hornets), the Carolina Panthers, and you cannot say *Charlotte* without saying *NASCAR*. Some of the tallest buildings in North Carolina are there: the corporate headquarters of the Bank of America,

Duke Energy Center, and Wells Fargo to name a few. Suffice to say, Charlotte had a booming economy.

We drove there to see it, to walk around the city, explore, and get a firmer grasp on what kind of city it was. It was about two hours away from where we were staying in Raleigh. We decided to start with Downtown Charlotte. We parked somewhere on Seventh Street and started on foot. The first time we took a look around, we thought the place was phenomenal! It was very clean, and it felt safe. Every few blocks or so we would see patrolling guards.

We found a public market near the train tracks. There we discovered that there were a lot of cheeses for sale, a lot of different kinds of food and coffee. LyRae even found where to get freshly pressed juices. From the market, it was about a block to the epicenter of Downtown Charlotte. We walked past a street where we saw the headquarters of the Bank of America towering over us. We kept on going and looking around until we found ourselves in a small corner of the road, almost like an alleyway. It had rows and rows of restaurants on both sides. After every few feet was a different restaurant with a different design, all laid out in this quiet little corner.

We kept looking around and just strolling. We eventually found ourselves in front of the Discovery Place where there were these sound mirrors that we played with. There was a sign that read, "Speak your mind even if your voice shakes." I know that sound mirrors were used in WWII, as an early warning sign that the enemy was coming. Each "mirror" looks like a dish and placed across from each other at a great distance. You can hear everything from one end, despite the wide space.

"Do you read me, LyRae?" I whispered into one of the mirrors. "Am I coming through loud and clear, over?" I held back a laugh.

"I read you loud and clear," LyRae responded from the other side.

"You forgot to say over." I laughed.

I saw her laugh too, and she rolled her eyes from across the way. "Loud and clear, over and out," she said.

Like Hannah mentioned during this visit, there was this big event called Taste of Charlotte. It is a three-day festival that takes over about five blocks of the city once a year, always in the month of June. All local restaurants displayed their signature dishes for residents and tourists to enjoy, but we did not find Brownstone's sandwich shop. I think it was during this particular visit that RJ decided he wanted to live in Charlotte too.

Nightlife in Uptown Charlotte is also pretty interesting, no doubt another reason that contributed to RJ moving to the area. There are so many things to see! There are six different theaters, and there is always a Broadway show on or a musical act to listen to. One of the things I found funny was the Trolley Pub. It is like a mobile bar where you and a bunch of friends can sit and pedal just like you would a bicycle and cruise along uptown, drink in hand.

As much as we liked our experience in Charlotte, it felt like the city catered to a younger generation and we were past that point. LyRae and I fell completely in love with Raleigh. It is the state's capital and one of the largest cities in North Carolina, second only to Charlotte.

We fell in love with the oak tree-lined roads, the warm days, and the short winters. If the weather was not enough reason to move there, the people were. People are happy there, and it shows in the way they welcome you when they meet you. Raleigh is a big city, big enough that you keep meeting new people but has a small town feel where you constantly run into the people you know.

What we especially liked was the research triangle, named as such because of the three major research universities in the area (who were also their partners): Duke University, the University of North Carolina at Chapel Hill, and North Carolina State University. Their location formed a triangle, and the park was right smack in the middle.

The park was established in 1959 and aimed to prevent the brain drain from these prestigious universities. It is eight miles long, two miles wide, and covers seven thousand acres. It is now the home of over 170 companies. If I ever needed to find a job, it would have definitely been somewhere there. Raleigh is, after all, one of the top best places for businesses and careers. We felt that it was more settled than Charlotte was.

We visited Son'Serae so many times and saw so much of North Carolina, we finally reached a well thought-out decision that we wanted to move there and live in Raleigh.

Plans to move became solid and set in motion.

We started looking for places to live. Like we always did when planning a move, LyRae and I would choose about four or five places and rank them.

To rank them, we would consider several things. One of those things would be the distance from grocery stores, the market, and the church. Next, we looked at the neighborhood and ask each other if we thought the area was safe. We'd check the crime rate. Then we'd look at how much it would cost.

Location A, it was a great place! It was near to everything. The market was close, but it was too close for comfort. We suspected that it could get really loud.

Location B, we did not like their tenants. They were rough-mannered people, and they cursed too often for my taste.

Location C, it was perfect but beyond our price range.

Location D, we heard from the neighbors that sanitation and waste management was a concern.

Location E, it fit the basic things we were looking for, but it was smaller than what we were hoping for. It came with a very reasonable rate.

For the move to Raleigh, an apartment complex in Brier Creek topped our list. It was secure, with gates and fences. The apartment we found was a two bedroom. It had a separate alcove that I could use for a study and the layout of the entire place was larger than everything else we had the opportunity of viewing.

We were really moving there! It was an exciting time.

It was around the end of June, just before our second wedding, that we finally decided to put our house on the market. Anyway, it was just the two of us and it will just be the two of us, with the occasional family visits. Son'Serae was studying in Durham, and RJ had just graduated was looking for a job. It was just one less thing to worry about before we moved to Raleigh.

We got in touch with a realtor, a very nice gentleman, who came and looked at our house. He went from room to room and looked at everything. After his inspection, he told us that he did not think the house will be on the market for very long. I thought it might take at least a month.

So we moved a lot of our things to the basement and started staging the house for viewers to come in and check. It was a month-long process. It got so hectic, a never-ending hurricane of clothes, furniture, and split-second decisions.

Do we keep this old vase our neighbor once gave to us or throw it out?

Do I want to keep, donate, or store my old, now raggedy, HU sweatshirt?

Do I want to wear this hat? I have not worn it for a year.

LyRae asked if we are keeping a dresser.

Are we keeping the washer dryer?

Are we keeping the refrigerator?

The more things we went through, the more surreal the whole situation became. It dawned on me how hard it was to let go of the house my children grew up in as I moved from room to room, revisiting one memory after the other.

I entered RJ's bedroom. He had moved out quite a while ago when he left for college. It was still filled with most of his high school things. His posters of Bob Marley and the Wailers were still up on his wall. I saw the couch that he begged me to buy one day at Macy's, insisting he needed it so he can be more comfortable when playing games on his Xbox.

"This couch is perfect for my room!" he had said excitedly. "It fits in the corner by my window, don't you think so, Dad?"

"Mmhmm."

"Oh, come on. If Mom were here, you know she'll get it. She would say it matches the carpet! And look, it is on sale!"

We ended up buying the couch, and his mother did say the color matched the carpet.

He spent hours on that couch playing all sorts of games, and when I knocked on the door to ask him to turn that racket down, he would say defensively, "It is not racket, Dad. it is Call of Duty!" I chuckled at the memory and started taking down the posters. RJ liked his games. I remember LyRae teaching him that money did not grow on trees. He had to save up for the things he liked, including his games, and they were pretty costly too, about twenty to thirty dollars each.

I walked across the hall and into the next room. It was Son'Serae's. My baby girl, always the untidy one. When RJ moved out, he left his room clean. But my baby girl, she had the messiest room I had ever seen. The only clean thing in that room was her trash can. She cannot seem to remember to throw anything in there. I remember complaining about it one day when I happened to pass by and her door was open. Crumpled pieces of paper everywhere, around the trash can, never in it where it is supposed to be.

Her room was always color coordinated though, the color of her bedsheets always had to match the curtains. She had this small obsession with ladies accessories and had an entire wall dedicated to this. This wall of accessories occupied about three-fourths of the wall, and each line of accessories was organized per material, or color, or kind. The other one-fourth of the wall was dedicated to hair products. Lord knows what they are used for. She also had a number of hairbrushes that she accumulated throughout the years.

How many hairbrushes does one need anyway?

I looked around and noticed for the first time in years that my daughter's room was pink. Son'Serae had painted it herself when she was thirteen years old. She did a good job too. I remember going to the store with LyRae to get her the fuchsia-colored paint. She had requested for it to be hot pink. Well, she got what she wanted. It was pink then; it is still pink now. My baby girl knows how to get what she wants. I decided to let LyRae pack her accessories. I just took care of the books.

I was going down the stairs when another memory crossed my mind. There was a time I panicked when I saw RJ try to slide down the steps on a refrigerator box, pretending to be pulled by reindeer and he was on a sled. I panicked even more when he told his sister to "Come and try it."

Young children can be so carefree; it is scary sometimes.

I walked to my right and stepped into my study. It was my own personal "man cave" as RJ liked to put it. It gave me a lot of mixed emotions. I had both good days and bad days in this room. One of my favorites was when I figured a solution to a critical piece in our project that took about two months to resolve. I thought about the hundreds of phone calls I took in this room.

I wonder, *How many hours did I spend working here?* The room was already bare. I had already packed up most of my stuff and just left my favorite chair and some books to make the room look more inviting.

The house was on the market on June eighteenth, a Saturday. People came in to look around in the following days, and on Wednesday, our broker got an offer. We were surprised at how fast that happened. On Thursday, our broker came to our house and we reviewed and signed off on the offer. The closing was scheduled for the middle of August. All was set. We were excited.

That Friday we went out of town with our children and flew to Atlanta for a scheduled family reunion on LyRae's side of the family. The reunion was in Augusta, Georgia, on June twenty-fifth. We went back to Atlanta after that and stayed for three days, and then we drove to Florida for another family reunion, on my side of the family, this time on June twenty-ninth. The reunion was scheduled for July first and July second.

By July sixth, which was our twenty-fifth wedding anniversary, we flew out of Florida to Baltimore and drove back to Pennsylvania. During this time, the buyers decided that they wanted to change the closing date from the middle of August to July twenty-ninth. We were stunned. Not only do we have to move out, but we also had our second wedding scheduled on July twenty-third. To say that it was a busy time for us is an understatement.

Our broker had already settled on a pretty good deal, and I really liked him and the stories he told LyRae and me about his family. He actually reminded me a lot of Pop, LyRae's father. The negotiations went so well that we ended up leaving the new buyers our refrigerator and the washer and the dryer.

We really had not expected the house to sell so fast! By July 29, just after our second wedding, it was sold to the new buyers. Everything else in the house had to be packed up and moved, and we had to do it in a span of five days. Five days! We had to be out of there by the July 29. It was not too bad since we already had most of our things in the basement.

Unpacking, however, was a whole other story.

We signed a year's lease for this tiny apartment in York, Pennsylvania, that we had to move into right away. Most of our stuff ended up in storage. Most of these were the things that just could not fit into the apartment. We had not lived in an apartment for over twenty years. It was a very big change for myself and LyRae. A lot of adjustments had to be made in order to make living in a much smaller space comfortable.

It was a two-bedroom apartment and by the time we moved, RJ temporarily moved back home due to life circumstances. We all felt so crammed in there, from a 2,600-square-foot home to an 800-square-foot apartment.

It was quite an adjustment, but we had to stay in this apartment. We had to stay in York, Pennsylvania, because of my job.

I was still working for a giant aerospace company as a senior manager, engineering. I would drive to work a total of five hours daily.

On one of these drives, I felt a sharp pain in my lower back. It was a Thursday. I remember because I knew I had a presentation due the next day, and all I had in my mind before the pain was the finishing touches I had to do when I got to the office. I thought at first it was probably how I slept, or how I sat during my drive, or maybe it was just one of those regular pains you get as you grow older.

For about a week, I would try to do the back stretches that I remember doing when I was playing varsity basketball. Most of the stretches I could not do all the way, but I am certain I was able to do them in proper form at least. The pain would go away for a few hours and come back with a vengeance.

The day came that I was unable to ignore it. The pain, it got so bad that I decided it was time to go see my doctor.

CHAPTER 4

DEPRESSION

I went to work late one day. This was in March.

I finally went to see my primary physician, Dr. Suresh, about my back pain. It was getting harder and harder to ignore the pain each day that passed. I had been so busy that I could not make time to have it checked right away. The pain kept nagging at me, reminding me.

Dr. Suresh is very friendly and open. Talking to him about my medical history felt like talking to an old friend. We had a long conversation about my daily routine until I segue into the sharp pain that I had been feeling. He is a kind of person that makes you feel you can tell him the worst thing about yourself and he would still have something nice to say.

He was a family man. He had photos of his wife and children on his desk next to his computer. He said he had family in New Jersey and in North Carolina. I looked around his office. It was mostly cream-colored with dark-green accents, and there was a small bed in the corner next to the window. This is where he would do his physicals when the need arises. As I stare at the bed, we talked about my work and my day-to-day routine.

"Well, Doctor, I am a senior manager, engineering, at an aerospace company. I work in the services part of the business where I do software development and/ or testing for a lot of different projects. Right now, though, I work in the ethics department."

"How do you usually go about your day?" he asked.

"For the past year, I have been driving to and from work for a total of five hours a day, five days a week. It was during one of these drives last week that I felt a pain in my back. I thought it was nothing, like maybe I slept in an awkward position the night before. I thought it would eventually go away, but it has not."

When I mentioned this, he proceeded to ask me a series of questions.

"On a scale of one to ten, how would you rate that pain?" he asked.

"I would say, now, about eight," I replied.

"Do you only feel this pain when you are driving?" he asked.

"No, it also hurts when I am moving around," I responded.

"What do you do to alleviate your pain?" he asked.

"I move around in my car and try to find a position that hurts less or stretch it out, but I could never find one," I said.

"Did you take any medication for the pain?"

"I did not take any medication for the pain."

"Were you hospitalized recently?"

"No," I said.

"Any family history to this effect?"

I paused, thought about that for a moment, and said, "No."

"I see, will you stand up for me, please?"

We both stood up, and he asked, "I would say you are about six foot six tall, am I right?"

"That is right," I replied.

He stood up next to me and said, "I have an inkling of what might be going on with you. I am going to do a test to see if I am right. Now, I am going to put my hand on your back, just behind your shoulder, and I need you to stretch your arm out with your palm up in front of you and lift it."

I nodded in understanding.

"I am going to put some resistance on your wrist while you lift your arm, now go ahead and lift."

I did as he instructed, and it hurt. It hurt a lot. He saw my face contort in pain and stopped. I was starting to get a little nervous now.

"I am going to do another test, if that is all right with you, Mr. Thompson."

"Yes, please go ahead," I said as he gestured for me to sit.

He stood in front of me and said, "Lift your forearm with your palm up, while keeping your upper arm to your side so that your elbow forms a ninety-degree angle. I need you to lift your forearm toward yourself, while I apply resistance on your wrist."

Again, I did as he instructed. And again, it hurt.

What could it be? I was afraid. I hope it is nothing serious.

He sat down across from me, on the other side of the desk, and said, "All right, Mr. Thompson, you have tested positive for tendinitis."

"Is this something I should be worried about?" I asked.

"Well, it is treatable. Tendons are tough but thin tissues that connect muscles to the bones, and your tendons have swollen," he told me.

Scared, I asked, "How did this happen, Doctor?"

"They started to swell due to overuse—meaning, you have been repeating a body motion too often, and in this case, it could be your driving or how you are sitting down. Your swollen tendon impinged a nerve that extended all the way to your back, which had caused your back pain."

He continued, "I will be prescribing some medication to help with the pain and the inflammation, but you will also need physical therapy. I will be giving you some referrals. You can choose which area is more convenient for you."

"Thank you, Doctor."

"In the meantime, you really should not be driving," he instructed.

What am I going to do for the next six months? Oh, the timing.

I was already planning to move to North Carolina, although at the time, no solid plans were set in motion yet. My company did not have a branch in North Carolina. This was when everything was solidified. Plans had started forming. It was eventually all going to happen.

"But no more driving?" I asked, not realizing that I had said it out loud until Dr. Suresh responded.

"Less driving from now on. You cannot keep doing what you have been doing and expect to get better. You have to go to physical therapy, and we will reevaluate after six months," he informed me.

I am six foot six tall; and apparently, being inside a car while holding one position for five hours, five days a week, for a whole year became very uncomfortable, and this was the consequence. I was diagnosed with tendinitis in both arms, from the middle of my arms all the way up to the joint close to my shoulder.

I chose a physical therapy office that was just around the corner from my apartment and went to physical therapy sessions with a therapist named Jo. She is a very pleasant, very petite lady from the Philippines. When I met her, I thought she might have been too young to be working. I guessed she was not as young as she looked though.

"How old are you, young lady?" I asked jokingly.

She grinned and said, "I get that a lot. I am thirty-five, and I have been a physical therapist for ten years."

"How long have you lived around here?" I asked her while she helped me stretch my legs.

"Oh, about the same. Ten years. I applied for this job when I was still in the Philippines, and they took me on straight after college."

"Your family is in the Philippines, I take it?" I asked her.

"Yeah! I am visiting them soon actually. I am looking at March next year," she replied.

"That is wonderful!" I said.

I went through the same questions with her that I did with Dr. Suresh. She probably needed to validate the information for the record. She said something about a baseline. She then introduced me to some equipment that we will be using in the coming weeks.

We started with what she called deep heating modalities, which is an ultrasound that is supposed to heat my deeper tissues to facilitate blood flow in the areas of my injury and promote healing.

We then proceeded with some stretching exercises and strengthening exercises, which I had to do at least three times a week. I was instructed to drive less, and if I really needed to, I was allowed to drive or commute only three times a week.

I did everything that was required of me by my physician. I had already stopped working. I went to physical therapy religiously and mostly stayed home the rest of the time. I lessened my driving, but I would still drive around locally.

LyRae started to drive more.

It is a good thing that we had already found a place we liked in North Carolina. Plans to move were already solid, but we also already signed a year's lease in the apartment in York, Pennsylvania. We were not moving until the following year.

Six months after that appointment with Dr. Suresh, he cleared me. Physical therapy with Jo had helped tremendously. It was around September that I felt something was not right. I could not figure out what the problem was, I only knew that something was not right in my body. It seemed like there was a problem with my legs and hips. I decided to go to the doctors immediately.

"Hello again, Ray! What brings you in today?" Dr. Suresh greeted me in his usual friendly demeanor.

"Well, Doctor, I was driving one day, and I felt a lot of pain in my legs," I told him and showed him my swollen feet.

He asked me the same standard questions and ordered an X-ray. After leaving the office, I traveled to the imaging office, which was several miles away. I met with another physician, Dr. Tolbert. I shared with him all of the signs and symptoms that I was having. He performed the X-ray. Shortly thereafter, I received the results. Dr. Tolbert said that I had bursitis and arthritis in both hips. He then sent the X-rays over to Dr. Suresh. Later that week I went back to see Dr. Suresh about my condition. He told me that I had both bursitis and arthritis in both hips, which was creating the pains in both legs. I could not believe him. I was extremely concerned because I knew what this could lead to.

"Bursitis and arthritis?"

"Yes. The bursa sac is the cushion between your joints and tendons, having bursitis means the bursa sac has been stressed and this usually happens when there is an inflammation from other conditions." And arthritis is an informal way of referring to joint pain or joint disease.

His voice slowly faded away into the background as he said this, I looked at the X-ray of my hips. He was pointing and explaining, but I could not focus. I was in shock. I got a grip and snapped back into the conversation.

"Does this mean I have other conditions, Doctor?" I asked as my heart skipped a beat.

Dr. Suresh looked at my medical results on the wall as if looking for the answer to my question through the exposure of the film that shows my bones. I held my breath in quiet anticipation for what he would say next.

Dr. Suresh looked at the results of the X-ray in silence.

"I am afraid you do have another condition. You have arthritis in both hips," he said in a soothing voice, then showed me my X-ray and pointed at the part of my hips that were affected. He answered the rest of my questions as kindly as he could.

He was pointing at the X-ray of my hip, saying, "There should be a space between these joints, but as clearly shown in this X-ray, yours does not. So it is just bone on bone. That is why it hurts you so much. If left untreated, it will get worse and you will need surgery. But we are still in the early stages. With some physical therapy and medication, we can avoid that."

When I heard the words "early stages" and "physical therapy," I let out a sigh of relief. I could still come out of this in one piece. Hopeful, I asked Dr. Suresh, "What can I do?"

"You really have to stop driving completely and put a lot less weight on your hips. Your arthritis was caused by mechanical stress. You really should not be driving at all," he advised.

I had to leave my job then. With this development in my health, I had to leave my job a bit earlier than expected.

I started physical therapy sessions with Jo again. I also went see Dr. Suresh at least once a week throughout the remainder of the year, and in those meetings, we would discuss the progress of my condition. My therapy sessions were not as successful as the first time I went through it. My legs and feet were still swollen. I had to keep at it. I had to push through the pain.

I would come home from my sessions, and dinner would be ready, but I never felt like eating. I was just tired and spent. My therapy sessions would push me to uncomfortable limits. Going home to a cramped home did not help to brighten my disposition. I would look around my apartment, and it put me in a foul mood.

I was often in a foul mood.

The apartment was just too small. I felt that I did not have space to get better and to rehabilitate. I missed my favorite chair, which was in storage. I missed my yard. If the apartment was bigger, I would not have had to go to the rehab center. I could ask Jo to come over and do home sessions with me.

How did this happen?

Why do I even live here?

I felt that my whole life was reduced to such a little space.

Will I ever be able to get back on my feet?

These were the questions that plagued me. Questions I never really tried to find the answers for as it was too shameful to even acknowledge them. I would go straight to my room without saying anything to anybody and just go to bed.

I knew I was not alone, but I did feel quite lonely. The sickness was mine and mine alone to feel, to face, to overcome. No one can relate to the pain I experience every time I try to stand up, or sit down, or walk. It probably would have done me a lot of good to get out of that apartment and just go ahead and move to Raleigh. I was pulled in different directions—wanting to move closer to my daughter in Raleigh, wanting to overcome the physical therapy and get better. We had a few more months on the lease. I needed to stay where I was.

Staying in a cramped apartment, my mind wandered on what I should do but could not and the inertia of it all frustrated me. At times I would go on days without moving. I would look at the hand of the clock as it moved. I thought that I was slowly wasting away. My days blurred into the nights. Sometimes I pulled the curtains over the windows and make my own artificial darkness since the sun would just come out and remind me of the things I wanted to do but could not.

I looked at the hand of the clock as it moved. I could see time passing, but I could not feel it passing at all. Everything was so slow and agonizing. Sometimes the pain was so great I would think of ways to end it. I would sleep sometimes, and I would wake up in pain only to see that just twenty minutes had passed. I sometimes prayed that I would fall asleep and never have to wake up at all. Only in those deep periods of sleep do I feel a sense of relief, but when I wake up, the pain would come back until I take my medication. I am my own worst enemy, and I wanted my enemy to die.

All my life I have been ready to approach different situations, always ten steps ahead with at least five solutions ready. Nothing prepared me for this. I searched for answers, but I was drawing blanks. I would lose myself in my own thoughts and spiral into a depression.

I felt helpless. I was being a liability to my family. Isn't it my job to take care of them? But there I was, stuck at home not able to do things on my own, not being able to do the things that I would like to. It broke my heart every day to be a burden to LyRae.

I felt so limited.

I would need her to drive me to and from appointments. I felt like I grew old too early and now I am useless.

She is the love of my life, and a woman like her should not suffer through this. She does not deserve to experience this. I should be taking care of her.

But then I asked myself,

What should I do about this?

What can I do about this?

The answer that always comes out the same.

Nothing.

I questioned my faith. *I do not deserve this.*

I was a productive member of society. I have helped make the world a better place with the technology I had helped develop during my career, along with founding a church. This is how I am repaid?

The thought of it all angered me, only this time the anger is directed at myself for being so worthless now. I feel ashamed. I feel ashamed for my wife for having to go through this because of me. Small apartment, worthless man. This woman deserves better. I am disgusted with myself.

In my periods of solitude in between appointments, I would not go out of my room for days, not even to eat. LyRae would come into the bedroom from time to time trying to get me out of bed. I did not mean to ignore her. I just could not muster enough will to talk or to move.

"Ray, honey," I heard her call out to me from the kitchen one day, "it is time for breakfast."

I did not answer. I could not answer. I did not want to answer.

I heard the bedroom door open slowly. Her voice was closer. "Ray, let us get some food in you. Come on, you need it."

Some days, I manage to get up. Some days, I do not. That day I could not.

"Later," I said curtly.

"But, honey, you have not eaten in almost twenty-four hours," she said.

I saw her face, and she looked like she was at her wit's end. That beautiful face should not look like that. She should be smiling, but I could not make her smile. All I can see on her face was worry, as she is trying, and failing, to figure out how to make me feel better, how to help me. I tried to get up for her, but the pain just pinned me down, and nothing else mattered.

I need this pain to go away. I need everyone to go away. I need to go away.

I surrendered to the pain, to the darkness. I let it consume me.

I heard her sigh a deep sigh. "If you are not ready, I can leave it on the table for you," she said as she walked away.

One Sunday, LyRae told me to get ready for church. At this time, church was held in my apartment. I thought about the people who would be arriving, and I just could not muster up enough energy or courage to face anyone. I could not pretend to be faithful when I am at a point of just letting go.

On really bad days LyRae would try other things to get me out of bed. This one day, she came in and just handed me the phone. "It is Mom. She wants to talk to you about Thanksgiving."

I looked at her defiantly, like a child would when they refuse to eat vegetables. I took the phone reluctantly and talked to Mom for a minute. "Mom, now is not a good time for—"

"Ray, you are still coming over for Thanksgiving weekend, right?" she interrupted. "You know how I look forward to seeing you, LyRae, and the children every year."

Thanksgiving in New Jersey, we did that every year. Until that day that I heard Mom's voice on the phone, everything before my illness had felt like a completely different life, that it was lived by someone else.

I felt guilty for wanting to avoid her call. "Of course we are coming to see you, Mom. We will talk again soon." I hung up the phone.

Am I going to be well enough to go to New Jersey for Thanksgiving? Am I going to feel like spending some time with the family? I do not want to talk about my illness. I do not want them to see me this way. I cannot even bring myself to take a shower or clean up. How would that go?

Oh, hi, Mom. Hi, everyone. How am I doing? I will tell you how I am doing. I do not have a job. I live in a crummy little apartment. I cannot even drive myself five blocks to get my own prescription.

That will not go over well.

I tried to look at my situation in a different light.

LyRae deserves better than this. I have to try harder. I have to get better. I thought about the life of Job. He had lost everything. Everyone died around him, but he stayed faithful to God, and everything came back tenfold.

Maybe this is a test.

The Lord is putting me through this, and so He is also helping me. He would never leave me, nor forsake me. He would not put me through trials without providing guidance.

With Jo's help, I had managed to stop the swelling in my legs and feet. We stopped it from swelling more, but we could not completely get it back to normal. Still, I did not stop going, I was very religious about going to therapy.

I slowly started coming out of my depression. I simply decided to move forward.

It did not come to a point where I needed to see someone about it, but it came very close. Hearing from my mother-in-law was the wake-up call I needed. That I had a life, a reminder that I had something to look forward to. A reminder that although I am alone in my pain, there are people who care for me and that I care for them too.

I thought, *The illness will pass, and I can make myself better.* Get a job? It was just a job. I thought that I can find another one, as soon as I was able. What is more, it might just be in North Carolina. I resolved to start looking as soon as I was allowed.

I came out of my depression, but I was still sick. My legs still hurt; my back hurt. My appetite was still off, and as a result, I did not have much energy to go around with. I started to do normal things, like join LyRae for meals, but I could barely eat anything. But I did show up for Thanksgiving and enjoyed my time with my family.

I barely ate anything for two months. I started losing weight.

Come December, I had started to feel something strange in my abdomen. It felt bloated, and you could see, it showed swelling from the outside. It felt like there was some liquid buildup that caused the swelling, and it moved around whichever way I moved. The swelling in my legs and feet had gotten worse, not better. I thought I should probably see Dr. Suresh again as soon as I could and get it checked.

I was given Lasix before, a water pill. It is used to treat fluid retention and prevents the body from absorbing too much salt. When I saw Dr.

Suresh about my legs and feet again, he increased the dosage. He told me to keep an eye on it and see him again in a week.

When I got home that same day, LyRae had asked me if I told my doctor about everything else, such as my depression, my loss of appetite, the swelling in my abdomen. I told her no, I had not.

Why not? I did not think it mattered. I was just depressed. I did not feel like eating. I never thought that could be a symptom of anything. As for the swelling, I thought that might go away on its own. After I told her no, I had not told my doctor everything else, this was when she made a decision to come to all my future appointments.

"I am going with you to your next appointment. When is it?" she asked.

"It is next week. You do not have to come. I can go on my own," I told her.

"I am sure you can go on your own, but I cannot trust you to tell the doctor everything. I am coming with you. I have to make sure you tell him everything."

So the next time I went to see Dr. Suresh, LyRae went with me. All the other times I ever went to see my doctor, I saw him alone, by myself. LyRae coming with me turned out to be a good thing because she explained to the doctor in more detail what was happening to me at home.

I introduced them. "Dr. Suresh, this is my wife, LyRae."

"Hello, LyRae, it is nice to finally meet you. How are you?"

"I am very worried, Doctor. Ray has not been himself."

"What do you mean?" Dr. Suresh asked.

"Well, he has been very tired, fatigued, and to be honest, he has been quite depressed. He barely eats anything. And now, his stomach seems to be bloated and he has had trouble sleeping because of it," LyRae told him.

He led me to the small bed in the corner of his office to check my abdomen. I lift my shirt for him to see, and he pressed on some areas while asking me how it felt.

"It hurts, Doctor. I can barely sleep at night because it is so uncomfortable. I cannot lay on my stomach or on my back. I struggle to find a comfortable sleeping position every night. It truly is a horrible feeling. I can feel the fluid moving on the inside of me," I told him.

Dr. Suresh ordered blood work and an ultrasound for me, the kind of ultrasound that needed for me to fast for six hours, so we had to wait before we got it. It was pretty easy, the lab was just next door to my doctor's office.

He called me that same evening at nine thirty after seeing the results. It seems the result confirmed his suspicions. He deduced that all my conditions were symptoms that had something to do with my liver, and he sent me to go see a gastroenterologist, a liver specialist.

He was sending me to a liver specialist. *A liver specialist.* All this had something to do with my liver? I did not understand it.

Dr. Suresh gave me a referral, and he assured me that although the doctor he was referring me to lacked bedside manners, he was a very good doctor, perhaps even one of the best. It was the holidays, so I had trouble getting an appointment. We were able to get one the first week of January 2017.

Before the year ended, LyRae and I had decided to go to a new church for the Watch Night service. It was in this church that I got a shock that scared me, but it also strengthened my faith in God. The service was wonderful, the music, the words of inspiration, along with the preached word. We all prayed until midnight.

After midnight, the pastor began to prophesy to individuals. The Lord spoke through the pastor and used her as a vessel to speak His words. At some point, she came straight to me and said to me, "You are sick in your body." She did not know me or anything about me. I did not know her either. She knows nothing about me. I had never seen her or met her before.

"You have to go through this thing, but it is not until death," she said.

LyRae and I left the church that night contemplating what that meant for us. I took it as a sign that I was going to have to go through more difficulty, but that I would make it through. I kept this thought in mind as I waited for my appointment with my new doctor.

When it was finally time for my appointment on January third, LyRae drove me to the doctor's office. Dr. Skye was a tall man with gray hair and blue eyes. He was very brusque and always went straight to the point with his questions and his answers. He looked weathered, like he had seen enough tragedies to last him a lifetime. We discussed all of my conditions and went through another series of questions.

"Do you have difficulty breathing?"

"No, but I cannot get comfortable lying down."

"Any loss of appetite?"

"Yes, I cannot bring myself to eat anything."

"Does your abdomen hurt to touch?"

"Yes."

"Any nausea or vomiting?"

"Sometimes I feel like throwing up, but I do not. Sometimes, though, I actually do."

"Any heartburn?"

"No."

Dr. Skye ordered some extensive lab work, along with an ultrasound and an endoscopy.

"But we just did that," LyRae told him.

Yes, didn't we just do that? I thought.

"I am looking for something specific, so I need a specific type of blood work and a specific type of ultrasound."

Oh.

Over the course of the next three weeks, I got the tests that Dr. Skye had ordered. The endoscopy was easy. They put me to sleep! They gave me some short-acting medication for the procedure through an IV, and I just woke up with a scratchy throat. I am not sure if it was actually scratchy or just a reaction I thought I should have had after having a tube down my throat. Dr. Skye needed the results to check what was going on in my entire digestive tract. This was when they sent a camera down my throat.

The results from my lab work and ultrasound told us that there was indeed some fluid in my abdomen that was causing my discomfort. Dr. Skye had his office set an appointment for me in the imaging department of WellSpan York Hospital so I can have the fluid from my abdomen drained for preliminary testing. He wanted to know if there was an infection in the fluid.

We did not have to wait long for the appointment to be arranged, by the eleventh of January, my first paracentesis was done. We drove to WellSpan York Hospital and went to the imaging department as instructed so we could have the fluid from my abdomen drained. First, they took an ultrasound, then they laid me down on one of the beds.

The doctor who was about to do the procedure said, "Mr. Thompson, I need you to stay still for this. I am going to insert a needle on one side of your abdomen for the procedure. This procedure is called a paracentesis."

I nodded in understanding. The needle he was using was similar to the kind of needle that is used when you give blood, that needle was connected to a tube to drain, which was connected to a container that collects the fluid.

"How many children did you say you had, Mr. Thompson?" he asked, trying unsuccessfully to distract me from the impending pain.

"We have two, a boy and a girl. They are both adults now," I told him. "Doctor, how long have you been working here?"

"I have been working here for about seven years now," he answered.

He used an ultrasound to make a mark where the needle will be going through, cleaned the area, and then I felt a sharp pain on my skin when he punctured it with the needle. I tried my best to lay still as he was doing this on the side of my abdomen. In a few moments, the container started filling up with about a liter of fluid.

I was confounded. *That came out of me?* It was a translucent kind of amber-colored liquid that sort of looked like beer.

"All right, nice and easy," the doctor said as he expertly detached the needle from my body.

The doctor informed us that they will be taking my fluid to the lab for preliminary testing and sending the results to my doctor. After this, LyRae and I left the hospital and headed back home.

I went home feeling a little bit better, simply because there was progress. I was worried about the cause of all the things that were happening to me. I have been a healthy eater. I conscientiously avoided fast food and fried food. I did not drink any alcohol, much less smoked, even in my younger years. I speculated about what might have caused this and could not figure it out.

I was dumbfounded. My liver was failing to do its job. My body was absorbing my fluids. I was feeling more or less the same. I was tired all the time. I had no energy. I still had no appetite.

About a week and a half after my first paracentesis, I felt the same pain from before. I suspected that it was the same fluid in my abdomen, the same fluid that Dr. Skye said would return. As instructed, I notified him immediately.

He had given us a direct line to use, and we called it right away. He answered after the third ring. "Dr. Skye, it is Ray Thompson. I think the fluid is back because the pain is the same from last week."

"We already set up an appointment for you at the imaging department for about a week from now," he told me.

"Yes, we do have an appointment, I understand. But the pain is worrisome or I would not have called," I told him.

"I see. If you feel you need to have it drained right away, you can go directly to the emergency department. They should be able to do the procedure for you there."

LyRae and I got ready fairly quickly. I really wanted to have the fluid drained. The discomfort was almost too much to bear. We took Dr. Skye's advice and went to the emergency department.

I went through the whole procedure all over again, but this time they drained four liters of fluid. We planned to see Dr. Skye in the near future.

Dr. Skye told LyRae and me the following, "I am going to call the imaging department and schedule you in for a series of weekly appointments. I will see you on your next follow-up."

The weekend before the series of appointments began, Lynette and Roger decided to throw LyRae and me a going-away party. Everyone knew that we were planning to relocate to Raleigh, North Carolina, on January 28. LyRae and I drove over to Lynette and Roger's home, where the party took place. Several of our close friends were present. I do not remember much about the evening other than sitting on the couch wrapped up because I was cold. After being there for some time, we decided to leave and return home. We thanked Lynette and Roger for hosting this party.

The first of these appointments was scheduled for January 27.

CHAPTER 5

FINAL DECLINE

It was January 27.

ℐ awoke. Aware of early morning air that had filled my lungs, I took my time as I slowly opened my eyes to a squint. I thought of how brazen I have become, daring to live for another day longer. To my amusement, I rolled to my side and gave an almost inaudible chuckle, finding what little humor I could find in these times. I thought if I could hold on to this feeling a bit longer, I could share this smile with LyRae. This was something I felt she needed to see every now and then. She was no longer in bed with me. I know she tries to wake me before getting up. I cannot remember the last time I woke before her. That will have to change soon.

Beyond the cool sea of sheets whose waves feel like they have been frozen in time, my hands felt the remaining impressions of warmth LyRae's body had on the mattress, giving me some idea how long she has been up now. It was then I took notice of her gentle footsteps coursing through the rest of the room as she started getting ready for the day ahead of her. Although my body has been facing the opposite direction from where she was, I could not help but shake off the feeling that she knew I have been awake the entire time. It is not easy trying to hide something from someone you've been married to for twenty-five years now, but I oftentimes wonder how many breaks she is giving me just to find out what I plan on doing next. I guess this was one of those moments. I did not want to move at all, and it felt relaxing.

After a brief pause, she stepped out of the room and uncharacteristically left the bedroom door open. It was a few minutes after that I could smell the coffee she started brewing. It smelled good, hazelnut roast, my favorite.

She is good.

I do not need any more hints to know when I have been bested by my better half. Not only did this confirm that she was just waiting for me to get up on my own, but also, my chuckle probably was not as inaudible as I thought it should have been. Letting out a small childish sigh of defeat, I sat up on the bed and my feet met the soft touch of the polyester carpet that occupies the entire apartment. I started contemplating how waking up this early should never be an everyday practice. It is strange, but in hindsight, have I not done this countless time before? The routine then advances with another visit to the doctor. Wash, rinse, and repeat.

How many more days like this? I blindly stretched my foot in the surrounding area of the floor to find my bedroom slippers. My toes were hesitantly feeling about the floor until the sweet satisfaction that came with cushioning texture of worn-out, yet familiar, foot soles eased the nerves that came with being unprepared to crack open your eyes this early in the day. I rose and lurched from one end of the bed to the other just to arrange the bedding. As if the promise of warm coffee was not enough to lure me out of my room, LyRae's criticality on how I might be unable to clean up after myself was motivation enough to crank a few unwilling joints in my body to do something productive once in a while.

Pausing just a bit to admire my handiwork, an image in my periphery stole my attention. For all the good folding sheets did to me, I was able to move toward the clear beveled glass door with a little more spring in my step. I saw a veil of scattered clouds defined in the rich tones of gold and fuchsia signaling the arrival of sunrise. A few moments later, a trace of leaden clouds that were once hiding at the edge of the horizon started to loom in closer. It is definitely going to be rain today.

I was able to catch a faded reflection of myself through the glass pane that separated me from inviting breeze outside. Unflattered by the disheveled visage that projected a ghostly image of myself before me, I walked the few steps to the bathroom, went to the sink, and splashed water on my face. I could not wait to have that hazelnut coffee. My eyes scanned the bathroom sink, and I reached for my toothbrush. I took the tube of toothpaste and squeezed some onto my toothbrush. I was careful to squeeze from the bottom and not the middle. LyRae had said something about this the other day. I started brushing my teeth, reached for the toothpaste again, and studied it.

Huh, she got the peppermint one again.

I felt LyRae gently nudging my shoulder. "Come on, honey. It is time to get up. We have to leave soon. You only have an hour and a half to get ready."

I opened my eyes, shocked that I had not moved a muscle. Everything prior to this moment was only a dream. *I cannot move a muscle.* I watched her leave the room again. *I cannot move,* I wanted to tell her. I could not speak either.

About thirty minutes later, LyRae returned to the room. She found me lying in the same position as I was when she left the room earlier. LyRae said, "Honey, it is time for you to get up out of the bed. You now have only an hour to get ready. We have to leave and go to the doctors."

About thirty minutes later LyRae returned to the room. LyRae found me the same way she left me. She observed that this behavior was out of character and must have realized that there was something wrong because she helped me out of bed and sent me to the bathroom like a mother would do with a very sleepy toddler.

"You have to hurry, Ray. We are going to be late. You do not have time to rest anymore," she said as she disappeared from my line of vision to get my clothes ready.

At some point, I came out of the bathroom and I went to the sink. I turned the water on and reached for my toothbrush. I stood there in front of the mirror. LyRae came back a few moments later, and I was still standing there, toothbrush in hand and the water running. I did not know what to do next, and I could not do it. In my mind, I thought I was moving but my body was not cooperating and was not responding as promptly as I wanted it to.

LyRae, calm as always, put the toothpaste on my toothbrush and guided my hand to brush my teeth; helped me get ready; patiently got me into my clothes, shoes, coat, and cane; and sent me to the car.

I began my walk to the car. It seemed farther than it usually was. Am I just walking awfully slow? It took me longer than usual, but I made it to the car. I got in and started to wait for LyRae. She did not take long. She was right next to me in the driver's seat in moments.

"Ray, you forgot your phone," she said as she gave it to me. She looked at me for a moment, and I could not understand why. She stepped out of the car, and I thought maybe she forgot something. I closed my car door, and she came right back. Maybe she heard a sound.

"Ray, put your seat belt on," she said before we started pulling out of the parking lot. I heard her and thought, *Yes, I should put my seat belt on.*

"Ray, put your seat belt on," she said again as we pulled to the main intersection.

We ran into a little bit of morning traffic as the sky started to clear up and the sun was slowly coming out of hiding. There was not anything to be heard except the hum of the tires running over the road. I knew she was worried—but not that it showed. I could tell because from the corner of my eye I saw her turn her head to look at me briefly every time she had a chance, every stop light, every stop sign, every crossing pedestrian. Apart from that, it could have been just another normal day and I was not exhibiting signs of anything unusual.

"Honey, put your seat belt on," she said for the third time.

Didn't I do that yet? We were on the highway already! I never put it on.

"LyRae, I heard you!" I said to her.

We finally arrived at the doctor's office, and we waited for our turn.

When the nurse called us over, LyRae started to help me up. I did not need help! I felt I could still do things on my own. *Just watch*, I thought. Upon arriving in the back, the nurse asked me to step onto the scale. I put one foot on the scale and stopped. The nurse said to me, "Mr. Thompson, you will have to step off the scale and place both feet on the scale." I got off the scale, and the nurse asked me to get back on the scale, this time with both feet. Then I had my weight checked. I had my vitals checked in the examination room, no problem.

"Mr. and Mrs. Thompson? Dr. Skye is ready for you now," the nurse said as Dr. Skye walked into the examination room.

"Good morning, Dr. Skye, how are you doing today?" LyRae asked cordially.

"I have had better days. Let us talk about you, Mr. Thompson."

Really? At this point, I should have been used to this kind of manners from Dr. Skye. It never ceases to surprise me though, his bluntness.

He started asking me questions. I could see him, and I could hear him, but I could not respond. He seemed to be speaking a foreign language to me. I could not formulate the sentences to give a proper response. I did not know how. I could not even nod or shake my head in response. Considering my obvious lack of verbal abilities today, LyRae probably predicted this earlier on and answered all his questions for me without a hint of hesitation. I tried to pay attention, but the speed at which the entire conversation went was simply too fast. I found myself paying more attention to the whites and blues of Dr. Skye's office, unable to keep up with the conversation. I sat there patiently waiting for whatever was needed to be done.

Dr. Skye then sent us to get another round of lab work done at the imaging department in the hospital where he knew I had a paracentesis scheduled that same day. LyRae helped me into a wheelchair, and honestly, I could not complain. I was exhausted, and it was such a great relief.

LyRae took me to the hospital for my appointment with the imaging department. I knew we must have driven there, but I do not remember the drive over. I just noticed that I was already getting my paracentesis done. The puncture from the needle must have brought me back to reality. I then got my blood drawn at the lab in what felt like half an hour later, and the nurse was telling LyRae to take me to the emergency department.

LyRae seemed to have agreed with her. It might have been the nurse's urgency or the worried look that took over her face whenever she looked at me, I will never know, but LyRae agreed. She took me to the emergency department in that hospital. The nurses in the emergency department room ran a few questions by LyRae, and the next thing I knew, they started to take my clothes off.

Why are they taking my clothes off?

I slap a doctor's hand away and try to get up. They will not let me. I did not understand what was going on. Why will they not let me move alone?

"Calm down, Mr. Thompson," the doctor said to me. Hearing that made me even more anxious.

What is going on? I wanted to yell at them. *What are you doing?* The words would not come out of my mouth.

A male nurse swoops in and tried to talk to me, to restrain me. "Mr. Thompson, we just need to check on a few things. We need you to stay still."

I did not listen, or I did not want to listen, and so I fought back harder.

I was confused, and I started to panic. Whatever they were doing to me, it hurt. It hurt a lot. I found out later that it was a catheter, but at the time, I had no idea what was going on. I thrashed about, hoping they would let me go and just leave me alone, until the male nurse needed assistance and more doctors came to help restrain me, and they decided to tie me to the bed. I remember that there were four doctors, one for each of my limbs. I saw one of them with what looked like a thin tube about to stick it inside of me. I tried harder to fight my restraints, but to no avail. They started to leave me alone. Perhaps they succeeded in whatever it was they were trying to do, or they finally gave up. I did not know what it was, but a few moments later, a feeling of calm washed over me. I felt sleepy and tired all of sudden, like all the energy was drained from me. This was the point when the doctors decided I should be admitted to the hospital. LyRae was on the phone with somebody, I am guessing Son'Serae, and was telling her about the development of my situation.

"Your father is being admitted to the hospital." She paused, listening to the response on the other line. I could hear that indecipherable talking sound of a person on the other end of a phone call.

"We are at WellSpan York Hospital." Another pause.

"I do not know how long it is going to be. We do not have anything concrete yet." Another pause.

She stayed on the phone for a couple more moments, until I heard her say, "Drive safe. I love you, and I will see you soon."

CHAPTER 6

CONFUSION

$\mathscr{I}$ come to, confused and disoriented. I look around, and it looks like I am in a hospital room.

What happened to me?

A young lady looks at me furtively from behind my wife as if trying to sneak a glance at me, smiling. She is not dressed in scrubs or a lab coat, so she must not be a nurse or a doctor here. She sees that I am awake and walks slowly toward me with apparent uncertainty. There's a young man who follows suit right behind her, and LyRae is also coming to my bedside.

"Ray, you have visitors. Say hi," she tells me.

"Hi."

I am still trying to wrap my head around what is going on. Does she want me to talk to these people? Why? Why is LyRae telling me to talk these strangers?

"Ray, say hi to the children," she says firmly.

"Hi, children," I manage to croak. My throat feels dry as if I had not uttered a single word in days.

They look at each other with worried expressions or in confusion, I cannot tell. As if on cue, they sit at the foot of my bed together, one person on each side, looking at me with great concern.

Who are these people? They must be in the wrong room.

The young lady takes my hand. "I miss you. They are trying to control your ammonia levels. You should feel better soon," she says with obvious care in the way she looked at me.

"We know this might probably not make any sense to you right now, but we are your children, and we are here for you, Dad," the young man tells me. So I am looking at my son and daughter.

Dad? Am I their dad?

I am looking at my son and daughter, and I do not recognize them.

I am feeling woozy, exhausted, and the room is spinning. I try to keep my eyes open, but they are heavy. I see a person who is walking into my room. He might be a doctor. I am not sure. I cannot focus. I am seeing two of him, and he starts to spin too. I close my eyes for a second and immediately feel better. I open them again, and I see LyRae back in the room. She is spinning too.

I can hear him telling her, "His blood work came back, and his ammonia levels are almost normal. He should be himself again by tomorrow."

"So what should I do now?" I hear LyRae ask the doctor.

"We wait," he says curtly.

I hear him walk away, and the dim sound of my hospital room door open and close.

The volume of everything around me is fading in and out gradually.

The hospital door opens and closes once again. There is only silence now. Silence and beeping monitors.

Sometime before the morning daylight, LyRae left the hospital and went home to finish packing up our apartment in order to receive the movers. Early in the morning, Saturday, January 28, 2017, I had two visitors. James and Carolyn came to visit with me. I am certain that I spoke with them; however, I do not have any recollection of their visit. I am not certain how long they stayed, but I do know that I was glad to see them. LyRae and I had met James and Carolyn through our daughter, Son'Serae. James and Carolyn became some of our dear friends while living in York, PA.

In between dozing off and coming to, from darkness to light, from being lost in my thoughts to realizing I am in a hospital, I hear a muted voice. It sounded far away.

"Daddy," the voice is saying.

"Daddy!" It is closer, clearer, and louder now.

70

"What?" I open my eyes, startled.

"Daddy, you are awake!" Son'Serae exclaims as she sits on my bed, a coffee in her hand.

"I am awake because you are just so loud," I joke.

I look around the room and notice LyRae is missing. "Son'Serae, where is your mother?" I ask her.

"Oh, you are normal again!" she says as she gives me a quick hug. "She is with the movers."

Normal again? What is she talking about?

"I want to talk to your mother."

She nods as I watch her take out her phone and dialing her mother.

"Son'Serae?" I call out with my eyes closed.

"Yes, Daddy, I am right here."

"Call your mother, I need to talk to her."

"I did that. I am telling you. She is busy with the movers."

"Already? How long was I out?" I ask, a little taken aback, unsure of how much time has passed, unsure if I was sleeping or just spacing out. I should get up and help. I look around and realize I am not in my apartment. I am in the hospital. I remember the drive here and seeing my doctor. I remember being unable to speak.

"You have been out of it for about a day. The doctors said you were in some sort of confused state. You could not talk, move, or recognize anyone. They gave you some medication to control the increased levels of ammonia in your system and your body has been responding so far."

"Oh . . ." I say as I process this information. "What happened? What did I miss?"

"RJ and I were here, and you had no idea who we were. You are so weird sometimes, Daddy."

I raise my eyebrow at her.

"Just kidding! It was an odd feeling though when you did not recognize me," she tells me. "Anyway, RJ will be here soon. He is with the movers too, but he will stop by here before going to North Carolina."

"I want to talk to your mother," I tell Son'Serae. I need her to tell me what happened.

"I called her five times already! She is busy with the movers."

"I want to talk to her though," I tell her as she rolls her eyes.

She picks up her phone again to call her mother. "I am tired of your husband asking me where you are over and over again." She pauses to listen, says okay, and hangs up.

"What was that? Why did you not let me talk to her?" I ask.

"Your wife is busy with the movers!" she says this slowly and loudly, not hiding her frustration with me.

I bicker with Son'Serae like this all the time. It is now giving me some sense of normalcy. It feels nice, like the sun peeking through dark, ominous clouds. There is no way I am telling her that though; I will not hear the end of it. She would probably bring it up at the most inconvenient time when I am angry with her about something, and she'd say, "But you said I was like the sun peeking through dark ominous clouds, Daddy." No. She will never know this.

A doctor comes into the room and hands a document to me. "Mr. Thompson, we have a document for you to sign. This document represents you giving us permission for a blood transfusion, should you need it."

Son'Serae is looking on and looks a little confused as she takes out her phone to call someone, I am assuming her mother.

"Mommy, the doctor just handed Daddy a document to sign," she says. "All right, all right, bye!"

"That is it? You could have let me talk to her!" I say with a small pretense of annoyance.

"She says she is busy with the movers. Daddy, this is for a blood transfusion. Mommy says I have to read it, and then you can sign it."

I sign the document after she gives me the go ahead and immediately feel exhausted. I let myself drift off, Son'Serae and her chatter slowly fading into a black background.

Sometime later, LyRae arrives at the hospital. Son'Serae and RJ has left the hospital. LyRae comes into my room and says, "Hello, hon, I am back." After LyRae returns to the hospital, she is met by one of my first cousins, Angeline.

"Ray!" someone calls and wakes me. This is the second time today. What is going on?

"What?" I open my eyes, startled again. *Angeline?* I cannot see clearly. I do not have my glasses on, but this woman looks a whole lot like my cousin Angeline.

"How's it going, cousin?" she asks me casually, like she came over from next door, just to chat. It is her all right, and Angeline is from Virginia. What is she doing here? I do not even know.

"Angeline! What on earth are you doing here?" I ask in disbelief. She is standing over me with a man.

"Val!" I exclaim. Val came too. They are both standing over me, smiling, waiting. I think I am dreaming. I must be dreaming. Angeline lives all the way in Virginia. It cannot be possible that she is here right now. I am in York, Pennsylvania, am I not?

"Well . . ." she says, prolonging, teasing. "A little bird told me you were very sick. Frankly, I was worried. So here I am!"

I try to hold back my tears. "But I am fine! I am not sick, Angeline. You did not have to come all this way."

"Yes, I did," she says as she gave me a hug. "I had to know you were all right, and I had to see it with my own eyes. How are you feeling?"

I cannot help it. The tears I am holding in refuse to be held back. They are pouring, streaming down my cheeks now. I can feel them flow from my eyes, one tear after another, unyielding, blurring my vision. "I feel fine! I do not understand what the big fuss is all about."

"You are my brother, and you got so sick that you landed yourself in the hospital. That is the big fuss. Why are you crying?"

"It is not supposed to be this way. I am sorry you had to travel to Pennsylvania to see me," I tell her, tears still falling down my face. I feel touched and humbled that she went through the trouble of coming all the way here. It felt really good to see her. I am usually the one who goes and checks up on people.

"We are family, Ray," she reminds me. "This is where I am supposed to be because you are my brother."

"Is anyone else here?" I ask.

"Yes, Val's brother came too," she says, nodding her head toward the young gentleman sitting with LyRae. "I heard Son'Serae was running around here earlier today, and RJ too, but I did not get a chance to see them."

"How long will you be here for?"

"Just for the day, we have to get going soon."

"You are leaving already?" I ask her.

"I was here half the day, Ray. You snoozed on me," she says as she laughs. "How are you feeling? I have been told you were tired all the time and that you need your rest."

I look at all the things I am hooked up to, and I feel helpless. It kind of feels like I have been in this bed for weeks. If I get up, I will not be surprised to find a depression shape in the mattress. I try to move my legs, but I do not feel them. I try to move my arms and nothing.

I inhale and let out a deep sigh. Rest, it is.

"Yes, I am exhausted."

"Let us pray before we go," she says as she takes my hand.

We pray, and I close my eyes. I feel like I just blinked, and it is the next morning already. It is just LyRae in my room now. Everyone else has gone, just as quickly as they came.

"You are awake! Good morning, honey," she says as she gives me a peck on the cheek.

"Hi, honey, how was yesterday? I am so sorry I cannot help right now." I nodded in the direction of my IV lines.

She looks at me tenderly and says, "It is all right, honey. I have got this."

"What did I miss?" I ask her.

"The children left. Son'Serae is in Maryland to meet up with some friends, and RJ left yesterday for North Carolina with the movers," LyRae tells me.

"Okay, great! When can we leave?" I ask hopefully.

"We cannot yet, the doctors are still monitoring your progress."

"How long are they saying this will take?"

"They cannot say yet. They have already switched your medication from an enema to oral medication now that you are able to follow directions."

"I was not following directions before?"

"No . . .," she says, trailing off. I can hear the hesitation in her voice.

"What did I do?" I ask her worriedly.

"You did not do anything. You could not do anything. It was like you were not there, honey. It was just an empty shell of you," she says quietly. "You looked like you, but you just were not here. You did not recognize the children or the doctor."

"Oh . . . I do not know what to say. I do not remember. I am sorry, honey."

"It is not your fault. Let us just focus on getting you better. You should rest."

I feel I have rested enough.

"Now that we have officially moved out of the apartment, where are you staying?" I ask her as I look around the room.

"I made reservations at a hotel a few miles from here. It is the same place the children stayed at last night, Hampton Inn in York, Pennsylvania. I can stay there as long as I have to."

She sees my concerned look and says, "I will be fine, do not worry about it."

"But I am worried."

"Do not be," she says with a wave of her hand, completely dismissing the subject of my worry already. She gives me a peck on the cheek. "I am going to get something to eat, I will be right back, okay?"

"Okay," I respond wistfully.

My confusion state, as they say, has lifted; and I am going to be transferred to a regular room. I do not require as much observation and care as I have been receiving over the last few days, but I am still tired all the time. I go in and out of consciousness most of the day. The confusion state has lifted, but I am only vaguely aware that my friends Earl and Joyce are here, visiting, checking to see how I am doing. I am happy to see them. I am able to talk to them for a bit.

I drift away again and wake in a different room. I suppose this is the regular room already. There's a remote control for the TV on my bedside, and I reach for it. I flip through the channels, and there's nothing good on. I turn it back off.

I close my eyes again. *Hello, darkness, my old friend.*

I wake and it is another day! It is a good day! I feel good. I finally manage to get up from the hospital bed and go to the bathroom with some help from the nurses. We take the IV pole that my medications are attached to.

Do I really need this many?

Should I be stretching?

I recall that lying down cannot be too healthy for the muscles. What was it that Jo, my physical therapist, always told me? Stretch every morning. This is not so bad. I think the medication is really doing its job.

"Good morning, Mr. Thompson." It must be around 7:00 a.m. The nice young man who brings me breakfast every morning is here.

"What is for breakfast today, Ben?" I ask him.

"Everything nutritious," he replies with a grin. "You have a good one, Mr. Thompson. I will see you around lunch."

"I will be right here," I say.

Hospital food. Why do people say they hate hospital food?

Eggs? Good.

Bacon? Good.

Bread? I like mine toasted, but this will do.

I go to sit in the lounge chair and pick up a book. The floor doctor should be here any moment.

My hospital door opens. *Ah, perfect timing.* The floor doctor comes in with his notes in hand. I barely went through my food. I did not feel like eating anymore anyway. Two bites and my appetite disappeared.

"Mr. Thompson, your vitals look good today."

I look up from my book and smile at him. "I feel good today," I respond.

"Let us work on keeping it that way."

"I will be right here, but any chance I can leave soon?" I ask with a grin.

"Not just yet. But let us hope so," he says with a soft pat on my hand.

"Look at you! Sitting up in the chair!" LyRae says as she enters my room.

"It feels great! Good morning, honey." It is a good feeling to be up and moving around.

"Looking good!" she says, giving me a peck on the cheek.

"Will you go for a walk with me? I feel like moving around," I tell her. I have been in bed for a couple of days, and that is too long for me. I have always been the active type, always moving around. I feel cooped up in here. I have to be able to walk around. I think I am good to do it at this point.

LyRae looks at my doctor, and he gives her a nod. With his go ahead, we walk out of my hospital room and walk down the hall. Once we reach the end of the hall, we start to head back to the room.

Sometime after my short walk, my cousin Evangeline and her husband Billy have come to see me. Evangeline is Angeline's twin sister. I look at them as my sisters, and I was a brother they decided to adopt when we became close about five years ago. That was around the time we started organizing our annual family reunions. The both of them are on the committee with me. Evangeline and Billy drove up from North Carolina, and again I am shocked and touched. Why they even went through the trouble? I do not understand. I will probably be out of here soon. I feel good.

"It is not supposed to be this way," I tell her, just as I told her twin sister. As I am saying this, my tears threaten to fall again, brimming in my eyes.

She moves closer to my bedside and says, "We are family," just like her sister did when she was here.

I feel my mouth quiver as I try to stop the tears that I feel was slowly falling down my cheeks. I cannot believe I am crying again. Evangeline asks me, "Why are you crying Ray?" I tell her that I did not know, but I am sorry that she had to come so far to see me. *We are family.* I am so touched that she came to visit. I have not seen her since the last reunion. She stays until they have to leave and return home in the afternoon. Before leaving Evangeline and Billy prayed with LyRae and I. It is a wonderful visit.

The doctors come in and inform me that I needed an endoscopy and a colonoscopy. For the colonoscopy, they give me a gallon of a mixture that they are telling me I need to drink before I get the procedure. I take my first sip, and it is disgusting, but I am supposed to drink a gallon. *I need to do this,* I tell myself. I manage to drink all of it, but I cannot keep it down. I start throwing up and finally had to stop drinking it.

The whole ordeal exhausted me. I must have fallen asleep. It is early morning. I know this because LyRae is not around yet. I am having that feeling that is slowly becoming familiar. It is that heavy feeling, and there's a thick fog in my head that comes up whenever I try to remember the last thing that happened. I must have had another episode.

What was it they said? I go into a confusion state. When my ammonia levels are high, it affects my brain functions. So, let us see. I remember I am getting medication for that, that is why I am here in this hospital.

I try to get up, but it is harder to do than it was yesterday. I had help then though. Maybe I can do it on my own, so I fumble around for those soft hospital socks. I cannot find them. Someone must have kicked them under the bed. My feet touch the cold hard floor, and I try to bend over to find the slippers. I cannot do it. I walk very slowly over to the table where I see a glass of water and drink it.

Wow, I cannot do this on my own. I fall back into the lounge chair, and the nurse must have seen me get up because she comes in and asks if I was all right. I ask her to help me back to bed. "Something does not feel right," I tell her.

I close my eyes and immediately fall asleep. I wake up and see that it is dark outside and my friends Lynette and Roger in my room. They are here for a quick visit. I am lucid. However, like this morning, something does not feel right. A thick fog in my head is threatening to take over me and my body. My friends did not stay long because it was getting late, and although it was short, it was a wonderful visit.

CHAPTER 7

THE TRANSFER

"LyRae?" I call out. I hear nothing.

I think I just woke up because I realize I do not recognize the room that I am in. I clear my throat and try again, louder this time.

"LyRae?"

"I am right here, honey," she says from somewhere in the dimly lit room.

"Where are we?" I ask her.

"We had to move to another hospital. We are in Hershey, Pennsylvania, now, at Penn State Health Milton S. Hershey Medical Center," she tells me patiently.

"Where are you? I do not see you."

"Right here." She continues, "My mommy and my cousin Kim are coming in to visit you today."

"That is great! When will they be arriving?" I ask curiously. I do not even know what time it is now. I want to say early morning.

"They will come in this afternoon."

"Okay," I say in acknowledgment. I get to see Mom and Kim soon!

I patiently wait for this. I look around and see a book on my bedside and decide to have a look. *Did LyRae bring me this book, or is she reading it?* I read the cover. It is called *The Unbearable Lightness of Being*. I skim through it and put it down. It is about a man having an existential crisis about whether or not to pursue this woman, not the kind of book I want to read right now.

"Good morning, Mr. and Mrs. Thompson," a doctor says as he comes in. He introduces himself as Dr. Robins.

"Mr. Thompson," he starts saying, "I have some news for you. Unfortunately, your liver is failing. You are going to need a liver transplant."

Good morning to you too, Doctor. "A liver transplant?" I ask weakly.

"Yes, a liver transplant," he says.

I am startled. I never imagined I would have to go through something like that. A transplant. It is hard to wrap my head around it.

"Is this the only way I am going to get better?"

"Yes. It is your best chance. You need a liver transplant."

A liver transplant. I did not see that one coming. I am shocked. I did not realize it had gotten to that point.

He continues, addressing both me and LyRae, but now it is mostly LyRae. He must have sensed that I am still processing this information. "His MELD score is at 36. This is ultimately the determining factor that he needs a transplant."

I try to comprehend this, but it fails to sink in. How did it come to this?

"With your consent for the new liver, if you choose to receive it, we will put him on the transplant list, and as soon as we get a liver, we can proceed with the surgery. One thing you should know though. You will be in the hospital for about two weeks post-op, and then you will have to come in for follow-up every few weeks or so for a year. You will have to remain in Pennsylvania for at least a year."

I look at LyRae in a panic. "I cannot stay in Pennsylvania for a year. Honey, did we not already give up the apartment? Doctor, we have already moved to North Carolina."

LyRae holds my hand and squeezes it to calm me down.

"I live in Raleigh, Dr. Robins," I tell him. I only know one hospital in Raleigh. "I need to transfer to Duke University Hospital."

Sensing an impending discussion, he excuses himself and leaves. "I will let you two talk about it, and I will come back later for your decision."

"Do not worry, we will take care of it. We will find a way," LyRae tells me.

"I have to take care of it!" I say in defiance. I am always in charge, and I can still be. I know I can.

"I will work with the hospital to get you transferred to Duke. I am taking over, and that is that. You are in no condition to take care of anything right now. Your job is to rest. I do not want you to worry," she tells me.

"I will take care of everything, LyRae," I tell her as firm as she was.

She places her hand on my shoulder. Looking me in the eyes, she asks, "Ray, do you trust me?"

Do you trust me? Of course, I trust her. She is my wife. I trust her with my life. As I think this, I repeat it to myself. I mean it. I trust her with my life. There is no need for me to be angry. I can trust her.

"Yes, I trust you," I tell her.

"Good. Then let me handle it. I got it."

The sound of someone clearing his throat interrupts us.

"Hello," a doctor says a little awkwardly.

I did not even hear them come in. Seriously, these guys can also be ninjas. They are so quiet and nimble. Two of them are here, one older than the other.

"Hello, Doctors, how are you today?" I greet him.

"Doing good! Thanks for asking. Are you ready for a paracentesis?" he asks me and looks at LyRae inquiringly.

"Ready as I will ever be," I say as I try to roll over to my side unsuccessfully. In an instant, he maneuvers me expertly, easily, to the side.

I try to lay still and brace myself for the sharp pain that I knew was coming. I look out the window, and I see all the greens of the tops of the trees. I wonder when I can go outside again. This is the same procedure from before. He inserts one needle on one side of my abdomen and drains the fluid, taking about four liters.

This is the fourth paracentesis that I have gone through. In the first three procedures I learned to expect the sharp pain as the needle punctures my skin. I have been poked around so much that this is not even a big deal to me anymore. It feels almost normal, sadly. I feel the same pain today, but more.

I feel that something might have gone wrong.

The doctor who did the paracentesis, a young resident, did everything his attending told him to. He followed the instructions of his attending to the letter, but I am feeling a discomfort that I never encountered in the previous procedures. It is something I feel going on inside me, internally.

When they take their leave, I immediately tell LyRae about my suspicions but she says it seems they did it right. They got the fluid out. It is true, they did take the fluid out. Maybe it is nothing. Perhaps the discomfort will pass.

Shortly after my paracentesis, Dr. Robins returns. "Have you made a decision?" he asks us.

"Yes, we are going to work with the hospital to get a transfer to Duke," LyRae tells him.

"All right, I will have the nurses get the social worker on the floor to see what can be done."

"Thank you, Doctor."

I see Mom and LyRae's cousin Kim arrive to see me.

"Hello, ladies!" I greet them cheerfully. "How are you all doing today?"

"Hello, Ray, it is nice to see you again."

"Thanks, Mom, I wish it were in better circumstances though," I tell her.

As I was having a pleasant conversation with my mother-in-law, a nurse comes into the room to observe my vitals. As quick as one could blink, a flurry of people are suddenly moving about my room in a panic.

I recognize two of them to be my nurses from before. They have been looking at me and then back at the monitor with worried expressions.

Should I be worried too?

They are discussing some things, but I cannot quite make it out. I try to focus my attention on their direction, but I cannot hear what they are saying.

I start to panic. What is happening to me? What is going on?

I scan the room, and I find LyRae standing next to me, talking to Dr. Robins, the gastroenterologist. I try to reach for her, but I cannot. She is too far away.

Mom and Kim excuse themselves. "We will be in the waiting room."

LyRae nods in acknowledgment.

A male nurse appears, seemingly out of nowhere. "Mr. Thompson, please try to lay still." I did not even see him come in. He gives me something intravenously as he says, "You are feeling a little disoriented right now, but you are okay." He types something down on what I have come to recognize as a dreadful little thing filled with bad news, and he pushes the laptop toward Dr. Robins. I am not feeling disoriented at all.

Dr. Robins then takes the platform, and he studies the information on the laptop. Eyebrows furrowed, he gets lost in it while LyRae finally shifts her gaze to me.

I ask her, "What is going on?" I know she hears me, but she just gives me this look that said, "Wait."

I try again, "What is going on?" All the sudden action in my environment seems to have rendered me quite disoriented and altogether exhausted.

I search her face for any sign of worry or panic—I got nothing. Whatever she is feeling or thinking, I cannot tell. I cannot read her. She had always maintained a level head, even in the most chaotic situations. She moves closer to me, leans in, and says placidly, "Your blood pressure just crashed."

"Well, what is my blood pressure?" I ask her, but she is not telling me anything more.

I asked her again and again until finally, she says, "Your blood pressure is now down to fifty over thirty (50/30)."

I wonder what this means? I have been going to doctor after doctor for the past year. I have had multiple checkups, and I know that the average blood pressure of men my age is one-twenty over eighty (120/80). Right now, I have less than half of that. I am pretty sure this means that my heart has started to give up on pumping blood to the rest of my body. I cannot figure out why. It does not make sense to me.

Why is my blood pressure fifty over thirty (50/30)? That must be dangerous.

I start to feel cold, but I am calm—the gravity of the situation not really sinking in yet. I know it must be serious. My nurses are looking at me in confusion. I suppose it is not normal for people in my state to still be conscious and continuing to talk to those around. I think back to what my doctor said I needed. He said I needed a liver transplant. All my symptoms pointed to end-stage liver disease, the final stages of a dying liver.

LyRae is talking to the doctor again. I could not make out too much, but I catch a few sentences.

He is bleeding internally . . .

Why his blood pressure crashed . . .
White blood cells . . .
Platelets . . .
Four doses . . .

I am bleeding internally. Did I hear that right? I close my eyes, and I fight harder to listen. I hear someone telling LyRae, "We nicked a muscle during his last paracentesis. This is what is causing the internal bleeding. His blood did not clot, so no one could have known he was bleeding."

"You nicked a muscle?" LyRae asks calmly, unfazed.

I on the other hand, am a little shocked. I recall the resident from my earlier paracentesis. I knew something was not right.

"It appears that he is bleeding internally. Our first route is to give him extra blood and platelets to get his blood to clot. I do not want to open him up with his blood so thin. I already had one of the nurses start this."

I let out a big sigh. I guess LyRae heard this because she is looking at me calmly and trying to tell me with one look that everything was going to be okay. In that moment, as everyone around us is rushing about, moving me to the ICU, I could only see her and everyone else in the background is just a blur. I am looking at my wife. I believe her. I have faith.

A few hours later, I call my cousin Evangeline. She is a nurse in North Carolina. I tell her how my blood pressure crashed.

"What did they say your BP was?" she asks.

"Fifty over thirty (50/30)."

"Are you serious? Ray, you cannot be serious," she says, incredulous.

"Yes, I am serious! That is what they told me. That is what LyRae said too."

"If that is true, you should be either dead or in a coma. You should not even be able to talk, let alone call me and tell me about it!"

That explains why the nurses were looking at me so strangely.

It was impossible.

It was a miracle.

On Friday LyRae continued working with the hospital social worker on making reservations for me to transfer to Duke University Hospital. LyRae was faced with reviewing a lot of paperwork regarding the transfer. Along with managing the paperwork, the doctor spoke with LyRae about my condition. The doctor said that the hospital could not transfer me until

I was stable. Therefore, the hospital staff continued to monitor me for the remainder the day.

Saturday arrived, and I had remained stable through the day before and overnight. LyRae was pleased with the state of my condition. Later on in the morning, Joyce and Earl arrived at the hospital for a visit. I was so pleased to see them both. We all laughed and talked together. During the visit, LyRae asked Earl if he would shave me. Earl shaved me. I felt like a new person after the shave. I thanked Earl for shaving me, and he said, "No problem." Joyce and Earl continued with their visit a little while longer and then they left.

Later on that day Lynette, Roger, and little Roger came to the hospital to visit. We enjoyed one another while laughing and talking. We talked a lot about all of our time in York, Pennsylvania, now that we were moving to Raleigh, North Carolina. We reflected upon all of the good times we had together as one big happy family. LyRae and I told them that we will miss them dearly. Lynette said, "We wanted to visit with you before you left tonight to fly to Raleigh, North Carolina." After their visit, they left.

CHAPTER 8

FLIGHT

"*M*r. Thompson, your ride is here."

I wake up with a startled look on my face. *My what?*

"Mr. Thompson, your ride is here," the nurse says again, gesturing to the door.

"We are your medical team," says the man who seems to be in charge of the group. "We are going to get you ready. We will take you out of the hospital and put you on the airplane," he continues.

"Okay," I respond with a sigh. I am not sure what he is talking about, and for all I know, he might just be a dream I conjured up. I automatically close my eyes again and let my exhaustion take me.

I am not sure how long I have been asleep. The creaking, rolling, unsteady turning wheels of my hospital gurney is unmistakable. It is a sound that constantly brings me to awareness. *Where are they taking me now?* I wonder. I hear the familiar swoosh and thud of the hospital door swing open and close behind me. It suddenly feels chilly, like I am outdoors in the middle of the night. I can feel the cold air biting my cheekbones. *I am outside now.* A flashing light breaks the darkness that I have started to get used to. I want to open my eyes. I want to see what is happening.

Opening my eyes. It was once a thoughtless move, once an effortless action; it is now a painfully challenging task. There is that flashing light again. *What is that?* And again in continuous, steady intervals. I feel a hard, rapid jerk from my moving gurney, like a car driven fast over an unexpected hump in the road.

"Be careful with him!" a panicked voice says. It is a half scream-half scold. You can hear the authority and annoyance in her voice. "Sorry! I forgot that thing was there," a younger voice humbly replies.

I want to smile at whoever that is and tell her, *It is all right. I am perfectly fine.* I want to do this, yet there is a frustrating delay in all actions my brain commands any of my muscles to do. My eyes open slowly, heavily. I blink a few times and try to focus. Two people are lifting me off my gurney and into an ambulance. I try to remember why this is happening. It is a little hazy, but I know where I am going and the reason for the journey. It must be the night of February 4, and I am being flown to Duke University Hospital in the hopes of a liver transplant.

Awareness. Mine is so fleeting these days. I am conscious yet only slightly aware of why things are happening as they are. I am aware that I am sick. I am aware that I am in the hospital. I am aware, but I do not know why or how. I hear tidbits here and there but never the entire story. It is like starting a film when it is thirty minutes in and never seeing the end.

I would not be surprised if I drifted once again right now. I have been drifting in and out of awareness for the last five days, and I do not recall a single instance when LyRae was not present. LyRae, she is my constant. The only one that makes sense in all of this. I would wake, and I would think it must be late when I find her asleep in a chair next to my bed. Sometimes she would be talking to a doctor or a nurse, and other times she would simply happen to walk into my room from somewhere with a cup of tea in hand. She was there, always. This might just be the only time where I am "awake" and she is not here. *Where is she again?* I struggle to remember the last time I spoke to her.

"Ray, you are going to be transferred to Duke University Hospital very soon, okay?" I remember her telling me, and I remember responding in the affirmative.

"I need to go back to the hotel, maybe get some rest. I do not know when exactly you are going to be transferred, but they said they'll call me. I will leave then and drive to North Carolina," she tells me.

It is eleven thirty on February 4, and I am on my way to the airport to be flown on an airbus to Duke University Hospital from Penn State Health

Milton S. Hershey Medical Center. I am still wrapping my head around this as the ambulance plays its familiar wee-woo siren while speeding through the highways.

Why am I traveling in the middle of the night? I do not remember much, but I try.

LyRae was coordinating with a social worker who helped arrange all of this for me. We had to wait until there was an available room at Duke University Hospital to put me in once I got there and also for an available flight. This was the earliest window that we could catch.

I remember a discussion LyRae had with the social worker, that I had to be transported in a jet because it was the fastest option and it was also the most convenient option in terms of my health. I needed to travel with a medical team to monitor my condition, and a jet was large enough to accommodate the six-person team I needed to travel with and all of the medical equipment necessary to monitor my vitals. The distance from Pennsylvania to North Carolina was also an issue. It was just simpler and quicker to take a jet than to drive.

At this moment, I realize what a circus this must have been to arrange, and not just that, this whole thing. I cannot imagine what LyRae must be feeling right now or how much of a burden this is. I am truly the most blessed person in the whole world to have her.

"Has anyone spoken to my wife?" I ask.

"Yes, we informed her that we were an hour early. She said she was going to drive straight to Duke," another responds.

I hope she gets a good night's sleep before she drives.

"We are here," a third person says.

The cold air bites on my cheeks again as the ambulance doors open. They are wheeling me toward the plane now.

I have never been on a medical jet before, and I am actually quite intrigued by the thought. It seems to be a very small plane, but it does not feel cramped. I can see it was designed to carry a patient and three to six other persons comfortably. They lift me and the bed I am lying on, to what seems to be a steel bed at the entrance of the plane that they are using to slide me through and into the plane.

I am still hooked up to my IVs for all my medications and fluids. I can see them hanging in front of me. Something is attached to a monitor that displays my vitals, my central line, supplements, the works. My head is by the window, and if I wanted to look, I can see all the city lights from a distance when we take off. I start to look forward to that.

The pilot announces that we are ready for takeoff, and I can feel the plane start to move. "Good evening, this is Captain Lee speaking. Welcome aboard the airbus. We will be taking off shortly from Harrisburg International airport, arriving in North Carolina ETA 2.5 hours. Please make sure all seat belts are fastened and the patient is secure."

I look outside, we are moving slowly, surely, gearing up to move faster and faster. The friction of the wheels and the ground just get louder and louder until we lift off the ground. A few moments later, I feel that familiar lift. The one that you feel as the plane loses touch with the ground, and then you are a little deaf for a moment, with that sort of beeping sound ringing in your ears. I try to equalize.

I look outside as we fly over Pennsylvania, and all its lights growing smaller and smaller as we move into the clouds. It is a glorious feeling, flying. I look outside until I could see nothing but darkness. I guess I fell asleep as hours that I cannot account for pass, and we are already landing. I wake up to the pilot announcing that we are on our final descent.

I turn my head to face my medical team, and they are putting on their seat belts as per pilot's instruction. Everything gets louder again until we finally touch the ground. The point of contact upon landing was always something that scared me a little bit. This was no exception. I brace myself for that moment. It feels like forever until it finally happens, that loud contact of wheels coming from the air and onto the ground. It is very distinct. I feel the struggle of the plane slowing down against its momentum until it hits a pace slow enough to maneuver around the airport and onto its assigned landing area.

The plane slows down to a halt. I look outside and see that an ambulance is already waiting to meet us outside. My in-flight medical team swiftly unbuckle their seat belts, and with sure, nimble movements, they slide me over to the exit where another medical team receives me and takes me to the ambulance.

I am in a small, private airport in North Carolina, being transported in an ambulance to Duke University Hospital at two in the morning. In its usual loud and urgent fashion, the familiar wee-woo siren of the ambulance goes off again, as we drive through the quiet highways toward the hospital.

It is the same everywhere, isn't it? It is a universal warning of someone teetering on the brink of life and death. I have flown from Pennsylvania, and I am now in North Carolina. I have flown with a 50/50 chance of survival, but I am still alive.

CHAPTER 9

VISITING HOURS

LyRae

Whenever someone asks me what happened to my husband, I always go back to the day things really started to go downhill.

January 27. I remember it like it was yesterday. It was a Friday.

It was the day of my husband's appointment with his doctor.

I cannot say I was looking forward to it, but the sooner someone told me how to make him well, the better. We were getting the results of his lab work, and other tests that day.

It was 8:00 a.m., and I had to get ready. I would always wake two hours before we have to leave, mostly because the hot water runs out and my sweet Ray had been very weak at the time. He moves so slowly, and I must adjust in order to make it to appointments on time.

His routine was as follows:

Get up.

Rest.

Shower.

Rest.

Get dressed.

Rest.

Leave.

Every normal activity for a person to do has become difficult to accomplish. Difficult, yes. It was still doable. What we were doing then was a time-consuming process, but it worked for us, and I knew that it was temporary.

I have always been a patient person, and I am no stranger to change. I looked around at the apartment that we've been living in for the past six months. It was a very big change from the house we used to live in.

It is so different that I think it depressed Ray for some time. Maybe it was his condition that contributed to the depression, but part of me thinks this apartment was also cause for it. He was very much open to discussing his feelings about it. He did not have good feelings about it.

I tried to make it as homey as I could, given the limited amount of space. I woke him before I walked over to the kitchen, and I smiled a little to myself as I begin brewing his favorite coffee. *This should motivate him to move faster.*

I left the coffee pot to brew on its own, emitting the lovely scent of hazelnut, to go back to the bedroom and see how he is doing. He was still asleep. I nudged Ray gently and he stirred, awake.

"Come on, honey, it is time to get up. We have to leave soon. You only have an hour and a half to get ready."

When I saw him open his eyes, I went back to the kitchen to give him time to get ready. I poured myself a cup of tea as I watched the news. It was dominated by updates regarding President Trump. The state department was just ousted by the Trump administration that week.

I went back to the room, and Ray was still in the exact same spot he was in when I left him the first time I woke him up. This time I said, "Honey, it is time for you to get up." I left the room for the second time.

I switched the channel to weather, they were saying it was going to be sunny some parts of the day but cloudy for most of it. *It is a quiet Friday morning*, I thought.

It was too quiet.

No sound of footsteps, no sound of the shower running. I checked the time. *What is taking him so long?*

I went to check on him, which was the third time. He was still in bed! He had not moved. I walked over to his side. This was not normal. He had been slow to move, but it was never like this.

92

I was worried.

I slowly helped him sit up, and he cooperated, no problem. But without my prodding, it did not seem like he was going to move on his own. I help him out of bed and sent him to the bathroom.

"You have to hurry, Ray. We are going to be late. You do not have time to rest anymore."

I hated saying that, but it was true. We had an appointment, and it was one that I had been looking forward to, to gather information, to get some answers.

I noticed him coming out of the bathroom while I quickly put his clothes together. When I turned to look at him again, I see that he has not moved at all. He was staring blankly into our bathroom mirror with his toothbrush in his hand. He was frozen in time with the water running.

I was scared.

I put toothpaste on his toothbrush and guided him to brush his teeth and to put on fresh clothes, his shoes, as well as his coat.

"I want you to continue and walk to the car while I get ready, okay, Ray?" I said when I gave him his cane.

He nodded and walked slowly out the bedroom door. Before I walked out the door myself, I ran through my checklist.

Did I have my purse? Yes.

Keys? Yes.

Phone? No.

I rushed back to the bedroom and grabbed my phone. I saw that Ray forgot his too, so I took that and ran out of the apartment. As I stepped out, I saw him just getting into the car.

"Ray, you forgot your phone," I told him as I get in. He did not really acknowledge that, and he never asked for his phone. The last time he used his phone was the day before. I saw that he has not closed his door yet, so I kind of just looked at him to wait and see if he would.

He did not.

I stepped out, and just before I got around the car I saw and heard him close the passenger door. If I was not in such a hurry, I would have laughed right then and there.

I went back around, got into the driver's seat, and started the car. I told Ray to put his seat belt on. "Ray, please put your seat belt on."

I heard the familiar hum of the engine and pulled out of the driveway. "Please put your seat belt on," I told him again.

I stole a quick glance at him every chance I got. I do not know how he was feeling, or what was wrong with him exactly, and I was hoping the doctor can tell me. As I reached the highway, I saw the sky had started to clear up. I was so sure it was going to rain that day, but it did not, and it did not look like it will. That was another sign, I think. There will be dark times, and it is not going to be easy. At the end of it all, we will be all right and everything will go back to normal.

I noticed Ray did not put his seat belt on yet, so I told him again.

"Honey, put your seat belt on."

"LyRae, I heard you," he said, but he never put it on. I decided to stop reminding him.

I found myself thinking about New Year's Eve when we went to church. It was a new church that we went to for Watch Night Service that started at 10:00 p.m. that night, we had never been there before. We did not know the pastor. As the New Year approached, a few minutes after midnight, God moved in her, in the pastor. He used her as a vessel to give words to the people. She looked at Ray and confirmed that he was ill. She told Ray that he was not feeling well in his body. "You have to go through, but it is not until death," she said.

I believed her. I believed her words. I still do. I kept her words in my heart. I knew then my husband was going to be fine. I remembered when all of this started and how depressed he was, how he even got through that, I did not know. What I did know was, we can both pull through this, whatever happens.

Does he know how strong he is?

I had let myself take a deep breath and release it with some relief, remembering that everything was going to be fine. We just had to go through this.

We reached the doctor's office, and when the nurse called us over, I tried to help Ray up but he refused to let me. He seemed determined to get up on his own. He believed that he could, and I knew he could. It just took a little longer than normal.

The nurse needed to check his weight. She took us to an area where they had the weighing scale. Ray had only put one foot on the scale. "Mr.

Thompson, we need both your feet on the scale so we can get an accurate reading," the nurse said to him.

He muttered something, but neither of us could understand it. It seemed like he did not understand why both feet had to be on the scale. He had to do it all over again, take his foot of off it, and put it back again. As you can imagine, each time he did this it took a couple of minutes, until he finally placed both of his feet on the scale and the nurse was finally able to take note of his weight.

We went to an exam room where the nurse took his vitals, and she noticed that I was not having the easiest time with him. She said, "When you are ready to leave, I can get you a wheelchair so you can move him around easier." I gave her a grateful smile. Yes, a wheelchair will be a tremendous help.

When Dr. Skye was ready for us, he came to the exam room. I forgot how straight to the point he always was, like he did not have time for pleasantries. I did not mind that so much. He started asking Ray a series of questions; but Ray, given the condition he was in that morning, could not answer right away. I took over and answered all the doctor's questions. I also had a few of my own.

"What were the results of the previous tests that were performed?" I asked. I was informed that his iron was low, his bilirubin was high, and enzymes were slightly high.

"From the endoscopy, we found that the varices were inflamed, but there is no bleeding. From the paracentesis there was no infection. But from the ultrasound and X-ray, we found how severe his cirrhosis is," Dr. Skye responded.

"How often should Ray get a paracentesis?"

"Every week or every other week."

I proceeded to ask him a few more questions that had been on my mind. "Doctor, my husband has not been eating lately, why is that?"

"That is because of his liver," he told me.

"Should I force him to stay awake and eat? He is always sleeping."

"No, he should listen to his body."

"Should he take medication so he can eat? He has not been eating well."

"It would be counterproductive to give him medication for that, if he does not eat, that simply means he does not have room in his stomach to eat."

"Should he be taking liquid supplements? Such as energy drinks or protein powder?"

"That should be fine."

"Is it normal for him to be losing his memory and his balance?"

"Yes, that is because of his liver issue."

"How far along is his cirrhosis?" I asked. I knew he had cirrhosis, Dr. Suresh had told Ray this and Ray had relayed it to me. I just wanted to know.

"Severe," he said.

I sat silently as I processed all of this.

"I am ordering more lab work for you to get done. You can get this done at the imaging department. You have an appointment there today as well, yes?"

I nodded in response.

"I will fax over the paperwork for it," he continued.

As promised, the nurse provided a wheelchair for Ray, which made it easier to bring him back to the car. I drove to WellSpan York Hospital, and the valet asked me when we got there, "Ma'am, do you need a wheelchair?"

I smiled at him gratefully and said, "Yes, please." He left and quickly returned with a wheelchair. I got out of the car and took it from him while he took my place in the driver's seat. It took a couple of minutes for Ray to move, so the valet was ready, but Ray was still in there. I did not want to push him, so I waited until he got out to sit in the wheelchair.

I started to push Ray over to the imaging department. We had gotten there early, so we had to wait a bit for the scheduled paracentesis. Ray was out of it. If you ask him now, he will tell you he does not remember this. While we were waiting for our turn, he just sat there with his head in his hand. When it was time, the paracentesis proceeded as scheduled, where they took out about four liters of fluid.

The nurse assisting with the paracentesis said with a concerned look, trying to help me, giving me some advice, woman to woman, "I do not know your husband. But if he were my husband, I would take him to the emergency department." She continued with great urgency, "I would take him to the emergency department right now."

I agreed with her as I thought about all the things that happened that morning, leading up to now. Ray could not get up. He could not do normal things like brush his teeth on his own. He was slower than he has ever been. If she did not tell me to take him, I would have definitely taken him to the emergency department anyway.

I wondered if the nurse knew something, like did that mean he was sicker that day? He was not functioning normally, so much so that this nurse, a concerned citizen, someone who took a pledge to help others, advised me to take him to the emergency department. She was right. I was definitely going to take him to the emergency department.

First things first though, we needed to get lab work done. I asked the nurse for the lab work to be done as our doctor ordered, but I was informed we could not get lab work done at imaging. We had to go to the lab. No problem. The lab was in the front of the hospital, and the wheelchair was a big help. I could only imagine how long it would have taken for us to get there if I did not have it, considering all the stops Ray would have to take to rest in between all this.

The nurse pushed Ray to the lab, where we had to register before getting anything done. She then took him inside to get his blood drawn. I did not go with him, so I waited. The nurse came back to me with Ray after getting his blood drawn. "I put a stat on that since you are taking him to the emergency department. They should have it right away," the nurse said.

The nursed asked me if I was ready to go to the emergency department. I said yes. We proceeded to go to the emergency department. The nurse was pushing Ray in the wheelchair. Ray did not know his surroundings and appeared very lost.

In the emergency department, they use a triage method. I registered with the nurse over the counter and waited for another nurse to come to us and check on Ray. I looked at him, and he seemed to be fine. He was just sitting there with his eyes closed. He had his head resting on his hand.

A nurse later approached us to run a few questions by me and to take his vitals. I told her about the events of the day, starting with how he was that morning and the trip to the doctor's office. The entire time I was talking to her, she was also observing Ray. After this, she told me that he will get the very next bed available. I was not sure what she was able to find when she took his vitals, but I knew he must be sick enough to get the next available bed. We had to wait two hours.

A nurse called us into an exam room, where we saw a doctor. The lab work had not come through yet. "I will order more lab work so I know what is going on," the doctor said. When the lab work came in, that was when they decided to start an IV. The nurse tried to put in an IV but could not seem to be able to. She looked at me with an embarrassed smile and said she'll get another nurse.

She could not find a vein. "Could your husband be malnourished?" she asked when she came back with a second nurse.

"Yes, he has not been eating very well over the last month," I informed her.

The second nurse tried and failed to find a vein also. "I will get another nurse who can do this for sure because we really need to give him fluids."

The third nurse who came finally found a vein. It took a couple of minutes, but she found one. She found a vein through a crease in his elbow, she started the IV and left. A little later on the doctor came back to tell me that the rest of the lab work had come in and that it showed his ammonia levels were elevated.

"The medicine that we will give him is lactulose. It is administered only two ways, orally and as an enema. Which one would be the best way to administer it?" he asked me.

Ray was not being cooperative. He was agitated. I did not think he would follow directions if given oral medication. It was out of the question. "As an enema," I told the doctor.

"All right. I will also be ordering an X-ray. I want to see how his liver looks," he said. "Now, it takes a couple of days to see the results of the medication. Normally, people with high ammonia levels are admitted so they can be monitored while they are getting their medication."

He needed to be admitted to the hospital. He also needed a catheter put in because they had labeled him a fall risk, that he should not be getting up and going to the bathroom. I gave them the go ahead. Everything was explained to us before the procedure was done, but it looked like it did not register to Ray at all.

He was confused.

He started to panic.

He flailed his arms about.

He knocked everything out of the nurses' hands.

He had to be restrained.

It took three people to restrain him.

What is happening to him?

"Ma'am, we are going to admit your husband so that we can monitor him closely," a doctor said to me then.

"His lab work shows that his ammonia levels are high. This is why he is acting the way he is. It affects the brain and memory functions. You can call it a confusion or a fugue state. He needs to stay in a controlled environment where we can monitor him and control his ammonia levels," he explained.

I nodded in response. "Okay."

I took a moment and talked to God. I told him that I had complete faith in Him and I trusted Him. In return, He shielded me with an unbelievable peace.

I took my phone out and quickly sent text messages to our two children. A few moments later, not even a minute later, my phone rang. It was my daughter, Son'Serae.

"Hi, Mommy, what happened?" she said as I answered.

"Your father is being admitted to the hospital." I paused to give her time to react.

"What? Let me call RJ. We will travel up there as soon as we can. Which hospital?"

"We are at WellSpan York Hospital," I told her.

"Is it very serious? I mean, how long does he have to be there?" she asked in her usual rapid-fire way of speaking.

I did not want to alarm our children, but I knew they would want to be there for their father. I kept my tone calm, so as not to alarm her and cause a domino effect on her brother when she calls to tell him the news.

"I do not know how long it is going to be. The doctors have not told me anything concrete yet. More tests will have to be done."

"Okay, I will let RJ know, and I will call you when we arrive," she said.

"Drive safe, I love you and I will see you soon."

I looked at Ray, and he had calmed down. I tried to talk to him, but he was unresponsive.

He was awake but unaware of what was going on, unfeeling.

A couple of hours later, a room had become available and a nurse took us to one of the private rooms. I let Ray rest. I was tired myself. That was a hectic morning, and I was more tired than I cared to admit. I took the only lounge chair in the room and let myself close my eyes.

I woke up a few hours later to the sound of my phone. The children were arriving. I checked on Ray, and he was the same way, still fast asleep. It was eleven thirty in the evening.

"Mommy!" Son'Serae exclaimed as she saw me. I just saw her come into the room.

"Hi, sweetie, it is good to see you," I said as I stood up and hugged her.

"How is he?" she asked while looking at me, trying to read me, occasionally peeking behind me to get a glimpse of her father. I felt her trying to assess the gravity of the situation by my reactions.

"He is doing well. He is comfortable. He is getting his medication for his ammonia levels."

"What is that?" she asked.

"His liver is starting to fail. That is one of the side effects of it."

"And what does that mean, his liver is starting to fail? He does not even drink!" Son'Serae said in disbelief.

"That is one of the things the doctors are trying to figure out right now," I told her as I saw my son walking up to us. "Hello, RJ!" I greeted him, with arms open to receive him with a hug.

"Hi, Mom, I dropped off Son'Serae and parked the car. Is Dad all right?" he asked as he gave me a quick hug and a peck on the cheek.

"He is being treated now, resting, but he is awake. We can say hi."

We turned around to face Ray in his hospital bed, with Son'Serae already going ahead of us moving toward his bedside.

He did not turn his head.

He did not look.

He did not seem to have heard us.

"Ray, you have visitors. Say hi," I told him.

He looked our way and said, "Hi," automatically.

"Hi" without feeling.

"Hi" without any sense of familiarity.

He looked away and stared into space.

Normally, he would have addressed them individually. Normally, he would say a lot more. A whole lot more. My husband is a talker. He would have probably said, "Hey, man" or "How's it going" to RJ and pick on Son'Serae a little bit, saying something like "What are you doing here?"

I tried again. "Ray, say hi to the children."

"Hi, children," he said weakly.

Since his ammonia levels skyrocketed, he had not been himself. He was getting a little better though, getting a response out of him is a good sign, even if it was a mere "his children."

Son'Serae immediately sat down on his bed and held his hand as RJ did the same on the opposite side.

"I miss you. The doctors are trying to control your ammonia levels. You should feel better soon," I heard her tell her father.

Ray was not acknowledging anyone or anything. He did not acknowledge our daughter. He did not acknowledge our son.

I had gotten a hotel room for the children when I found out they were coming. I went outside the room with them and caught up with them a little as I handed over the room key. Son'Serae was going to see some friends in Maryland sometime in the next day, and RJ was going back to North Carolina with the movers. He told me that he will be at the storage unit by 9:00 a.m., and I told him I will be at the apartment by that time.

I almost forgot there was a whole entire world outside of this hospital. I had been so preoccupied that I barely had time to think about the movers. I was glad my children came. I spent the night at the hospital. I went back to the apartment just to shower, change, and pack up the rest of our things. I needed to get everything ready for the move. I needed to get our new home ready for when Ray gets out of the hospital.

RJ went to the storage unit with the movers. He had stuff there that he had to pick up because he was moving also, then he went back to the apartment to help me. I told him to go and spend time with his dad before leaving. While I was out taking care of things with the movers, Ray was doing just fine. In fact, he did well the entire weekend. He was very much himself when his cousin Angeline came up that Saturday. She had stopped by with Val and Val's brother. I had already gone back to the hospital around two or three that afternoon. He was doing well, just tired. He seemed to be out of it when we prayed with him just before they left.

He was doing well enough that it was no longer necessary for him to be in an intermediate room. He was still very much himself when our friends

Earl and Joyce came to visit on that Sunday. They are our friends from our former church. They stayed a bit to chat, had a pleasant conversation with Ray, where he genuinely had a nice time with them. They even walked with us when Ray was transferred to a regular room.

It was very nice of them to come up from Maryland, and they prayed with Ray just before they left. We held hands around his hospital bed and prayed.

Dear Lord,

You know Ray so much better than we do. You know his sickness and the burden he carries. You also know his heart. Lord, we ask you to be with our friend now as you work in his life.

Lord, let your will be done in Ray's life. If there is a sin that needs to be confessed and forgiven, please help him to see his need and confess.

Lord, we pray for Ray just as your Word tells us to pray, for healing. We believe you hear this earnest prayer from our hearts and that it is powerful because of your promise. We have faith in you, Lord, to heal our friend, but we also trust in the plan you have for his life.

Lord, we do not always understand your ways. We do not know why our friend has to suffer, but we trust you. We ask that you look with mercy and grace toward Ray. Nourish his spirit and soul in this time of suffering and comfort him with your presence.

Let Ray know you are there with him through this difficulty. Give him strength. And may you, through this difficulty, be glorified in his life and also in ours.

Amen.

On Monday, Ray was feeling better. He was in bed for a couple of days and asked to walk around, and so we did. I walked with him down the hall and back to the room, then he sat in a chair the rest of the day. Evangeline, Angeline's twin sister, first cousin of Ray, came up from North Carolina with her husband Billy the next day. They came in the morning and left in the afternoon to return home.

A urologist, a doctor who specializes in the urinary tract, came into the room to talk to us. There was something wrong with Ray's bladder. He was not dispelling any urine. This doctor informed us that his bladder will be better when he receives a liver transplant. I knew he had cirrhosis of the liver; I did not know he needed a liver transplant.

I noticed him start to slow down again on Tuesday. He was not as interactive, and he did not seem to want to cooperate with the nurses to try to get out of bed like he did the day before. He just wanted to stay in bed.

He was exhibiting the symptoms of his confusion state again. He was not quite himself when our friends Lynette and Roger stopped by that night. I felt that something was not right. I asked his nurse for an update.

"Nurse, has his ammonia levels been checked?" I asked her.

"Actually, we've checked twice already. We could not get a reading on his ammonia levels. Both times they were inconclusive because the samples were contaminated," she told me.

"I see. All right then."

I went about the day, as I normally did. I listened to what the nurses were saying, and I observed what they were doing. I asked questions when I did not understand and took note of everything. I rested when I could.

At that moment, Ray was drifting. I was not sure, I am still not sure, where he goes when this happens; but he is awake. He was awake, maybe just not mentally present. He did not acknowledge me. To him, I probably was not even there. He did not acknowledge the doctors or the nurses. He was being difficult again. He was already switched to oral medication, but it looked like he will have to go back to medication administered by enema, just like the charge nurse said.

The next day, a Wednesday, he spiraled back into his confused state. The doctor came in and asked him if he knew who the young lady in the room was. "That is my wife," he responded. He recognized me, but he was almost exactly like he was the first day he was admitted to the hospital. He was not very verbal, and he was lethargic.

"He has not been very cooperative today. We might have to start administering his medication by enema again to get his ammonia levels back in control," the doctor said.

Everything that was happening reminded me of that first day he got admitted to the hospital. He looked like my husband, but he just was not there. He was lethargic. I was reminded of how I felt that first day he was admitted to the hospital. That was really the only day I was ever scared. I shook it off and focused my attention on the doctor who was talking to me, trying to tell me something.

"I am sorry, what was that?"

"His disease is more advanced than we are able to control, so we are going to have to transfer him to another hospital."

"Where is he going? And, if we are moving him, is it possible to move him to Duke University Hospital in North Carolina?" I asked hopefully.

"Penn State Health Milton S. Hershey Medical Center, they have complete facilities there. When it comes to transferring patients, health insurance will only cover local transfers better than long-distance transfers."

I thought about that for a moment. It made sense, for that period of time. "All right, let us do it."

There was a whole kerfuffle about how the ambulance medical team felt more comfortable that Ray be intubated for his transfer to Penn State Health Milton S. Hershey Medical Center, but the doctor informed them that there was no need to intubate him because he had been given lactulose every two hours prior to the transfer and seemed to be responding well enough. He was given the go-ahead to be transferred without intubation.

So to Hershey, Pennsylvania, we went, my husband in the ambulance and me, I left the hospital before they did. I checked into a hotel first and got my room key. The hotel was right down the street from Penn State Health Milton S. Hershey Medical Center. It was not a long drive from York, Pennsylvania, maybe just about thirty minutes.

Ray was put in an intermediate room the moment he arrived. Patients in the intermediate room are given more attention. These are the kinds of patients who needed the attention. Each nurse had maybe only two patients each, as opposed to patients in the regular room, where nurses had more patients each, maybe three or more.

Ray had no idea that he was transferred. I thought he might be taken by surprise once he opened his eyes and sees he was in a different place. Will he realize he is in a different place?

No matter, I wanted to still be around when he wakes up.

He was already awake when I got there. He had asked for me immediately. I showed him that I was still there. I stood in his line of vision. I was always there, as I always will be. He seemed better. He was responding. He was interactive. I made sure he was calm before I left again.

The next day, we listened to the doctor, a doctor we've never met before, a doctor who introduced himself to us as Dr. Robins, tell us that his liver was failing and that he needed a liver transplant.

"Mr. Thompson," he started saying, "I have some news for you. Unfortunately, your liver is failing. You are going to need a liver transplant."

"A liver transplant?" Ray asked in a voice that I never heard before until that day.

It sounded weak, maybe even a little scared.

"Yes. It is your best chance. Because of the condition of your liver, you need a liver transplant."

Ray was startled. It was a complete shock to him.

"You need a liver transplant," he said again, making sure that was clear. "His MELD score is at 36, this is ultimately the determining factor that he needs a transplant. With your consent, we will put him on the transplant list, and as soon as we get a liver, we can proceed with the surgery. One thing you should know though, you will be in the hospital for about two weeks post-op, and then you will have to come in for follow up every few weeks or so for a year."

I already knew that Ray would not agree to this. I had already tried to get him to transfer to Duke University Hospital instead of Penn State Health Milton S. Hershey Medical Center the first time he was moved, but due to insurance limitations, we had to come here.

Ray looked at me, eyes wide with panic.

"I cannot stay in Pennsylvania for a year. Honey, we already gave up the apartment? Didn't we? LyRae said, "Yes." Doctor, we have already moved to North Carolina. I cannot stay in Pennsylvania," he said shaking his head.

I took his hand and squeezed it gently.

"I live in Raleigh, Dr. Robins," I told him. I only know one hospital in Raleigh. "I need to transfer to Duke University Hospital."

Dr. Robins must have sensed that I needed to discuss options with my husband. He excused himself and left. "I will let you two talk about it, and I will come back later for your decision."

"Do not worry, we will take care of it. We will find a way," I told my husband as calmly and as convincingly as I could.

"I have to take care of it!" he exclaimed, eyes wide, eyebrows furrowed.

This was typical of Ray. I understood it. I understood his reaction. He was always the one in charge, but he was never in a position where he could not be. This was uncharted territory for him.

"I will work with the hospital to take care of your transfer to Duke," I told him as firmly as I could, with what I hoped sounded like a tone of finality that I tried to inject in my voice.

I found his inclination to take charge, even in this particular situation, quite admirable. He had always been the one to take care of important matters, and I am there to assist and support. He was getting angry. He really wanted to take matters into his own hands.

"I will take care of everything, LyRae," he told me, being absolutely stubborn.

I placed my hand on his shoulder. I tried to calm him down that way, get him to look at me. "Do you trust me?" I asked him.

"Yes, I trust you," he said.

"Good. Then let me handle it. I got it."

Two doctors came in to do Ray's paracentesis. The younger one said timidly, "Hello," realizing too late that it appeared they interrupted something. Ray took it in stride and greeted them both. One doctor was older than the other. The older doctor was the attending physician, and the younger one was a resident. The resident was following the instructions of his attending doctor while doing the paracentesis. It was all very standard, but Ray felt that something was wrong.

"They got the fluid out," I told him. "It seems they did it right."

He was not satisfied with that, and shortly after Ray's paracentesis, Dr. Robins came back. I told him that we had made a decision to transfer to Duke University Hospital. He left to get the nurses to find the social worker on the floor, to see what can be done. Ray had always been in charge. Starting that day though, I held the reigns.

Shortly after Dr. Robins left, my mother and my first cousin Kim arrived for their visit.

"Hello, ladies!" Ray greeted them. I turned around and saw them.

I look at Kim as my sister. We basically grew up together, even lived together at times. There were times when I used to live with her and times that she lived with me. We just took turns doing that as we grew up. I was very happy to see her, and I was very happy to see my mommy.

Ray was cracking jokes, asking about everyone else and how they were doing. Everything was going well. Everyone was having a pleasant conversation. Everyone was happy to see each other.

Some fifteen to twenty minutes later, another nurse came in to check Ray's vitals, and she was alarmed.

All of a sudden his room filled with people.

When I saw his doctor, Dr. Robins, come in, I immediately spoke to him after my mommy and Kim left to go to the waiting room. "What is happening?" I asked him.

I had made it a point to always keep an eye on Ray's monitors. It was a combination of that habit and the doctor telling me, "Ray's blood pressure had crashed. It dropped to fifty over thirty (50/30)," that I had an idea of what was happening.

That was bad.

Dr. Robins was baffled that Ray was still awake. They were surprised that he was still talking, that his senses were in working order, that his body was still cooperating with him. Everyone was baffled. It is unheard of.

A smiling, talking man with a BP of fifty over thirty (50/30). It was a miracle.

I noticed Ray trying to get my attention. He had been trying to since the nurses and doctor came into the room, but I had chosen to just give him a look that said be patient.

"What is going on?" he asked again with now a considerable effort, his voice almost a whisper. Perhaps his body was starting to respond to the crash, or that was him already panicking.

I hesitated to tell him what it was. Given the situation, I was not sure how he might react. I thought, *Will he panic and make his situation worse than it already is? Will my telling him change anything?* I decided not to hide anything from him. I decided to tell him.

I told him gently, calmly, and I tried to make it sound as normal as possible. "Your blood pressure just crashed," I told him, hoping that was enough information for him.

"What is my blood pressure?" he asked.

Again, I hesitated to tell him and tried to avoid answering him, but in a fashion that was typical of Ray, he asked and asked again until he got the answer out of me.

"Your blood pressure is now down to fifty over thirty (50/30)," I told him.

They had nicked a muscle during the earlier paracentesis, and he was bleeding internally. They were not able to detect it as his blood did not clot. His white blood cell count was abnormally low, so he will be given four doses of white blood cells and platelets to help his blood clot.

I recalled when Ray said something did not feel right. I know the resident did the paracentesis right because they were able to get the fluid out. The needle must have been angled the wrong way for it to have hit a muscle.

"It appears that he is bleeding internally. Our first route is to give him extra blood and platelets to get his blood to clot. I do not want to open him up with his blood so thin. I already had one of the nurses start this," Dr. Robins said.

As I was taking all this in, I heard Ray sigh tiredly. I tried to convey as much of my faith as I could to my husband. *You are going to be fine.* I tell him with my eyes. *We are going to be fine,* I told myself as I walked out with his medical team. They were taking him to the ICU.

"I will be in the waiting room with Mom and Kim," I told him as they left. The ICU was on the same floor. They just pushed him to another unit. "Please call me when he is settled, and we will come over," I told one of the nurses.

Ray was right when he told Dr. Robins that we could not stay in Pennsylvania for another year. It was simply not doable. I quickly began making arrangements with the social worker on the floor, who, thank God, was extremely helpful and quite resourceful. She was helping me make my husband's transfer to Duke University Hospital possible.

She told me that she would check to see which airbus was available for us. She did her research and came back to tell me about an airbus. There was a company whose service was exactly what we needed. They have an airbus, an air ambulance of sorts, a plane, that Ray can take; and a medical team can go with him and monitor him all the way to North Carolina.

She was godsent.

Ray, on the other hand, was being himself. Although he trusted me to take over and work with the hospital to get him transferred, he never stopped asking me questions.

"Have you heard from the social worker?"

"Not yet."

"Well, can you follow-up?"

"Yes, I did follow-up."

"What did she say?"

"She said she will check if an airbus is available?"

"An airbus? Like a plane?"

"I am not sure, I am waiting to hear back from her."

"Did she say anything else?"

"No, not yet. I am still waiting for her to get back to me on that."

"Well, did she say how much it was going to be?"

"We have not discussed it yet. We are still waiting for our options."

He went on and on like that until I had to ask him again, "Do you trust me?"

He said yes. He said yes and smiled at me.

He knew he was being a pest. He just could not help himself. He thought the social worker was not moving fast enough, but truth be told, it did not take that long. Ray was just being impatient and trying to get involved. The transfer plans took one and a half day to execute.

A lot of paperwork was filed. A lot of phone calls were made. I have never signed off on so many things before. I filled out a good twenty pages.

I had to agree and give permission for the transfer and all its conditions.

I had to be aware and understand the risks.

I had to know that anything could happen on the flight.

Check, check, and check.

I took care of everything that day with the social worker.

A few people stopped by that Saturday in the hospital to see Ray before he left Pennsylvania. Earl and Joyce came back. Earl wanted to do something nice for Ray that day and decided to groom him. So right there, in the ICU, Earl shaved Ray's face. Ray absolutely loved it. He thought it felt wonderful. In hindsight, that was probably not a good idea. Ray's blood was thin, so if he got a cut, he might not have stopped bleeding, I do not know. The doctors did get his blood under control after his blood pressure crashed. The blood transfusion had worked. Our friends just wanted to wish us well, and they all wanted to pray with us before we left Pennsylvania. The doctor had said that if Ray remained stable, we can go ahead and transfer to Duke the following day.

Ray was already accepted at Duke, so that same day, all we had to do was wait for a room to become available at Duke. It was one of the more relaxing days we had since he was admitted. Roger and Lynette, with their son little Roger, stopped by that afternoon. They wanted to see us before we left for North Carolina. Ray did not know this, but that was Roger and Lynette's second visit. Ray was lucid and was interacting with them just fine. It was a very pleasant visit. Ray laughed and talked about his time with them, how their friendship began, given that our time with them was coming to an end. We met Roger and Lynette through our son, RJ. Lynette had observed our son at the local high school, Northeastern High School. Lynette thought our son was well mannered. Lynette came to his high school graduation party to share her thoughts with LyRae and I, and we were pleased to hear this information. From that point forward, we became friends. Before Roger, Lynette and little Roger left they prayed with LyRae and I.

We eventually received a phone call that a room had become available at Duke University Hospital, but the airbus crew had to fly over to Hershey, Pennsylvania, and that took a while. I told our friends that Ray will be transferred at 12:30 a.m.

When our friends left and the day was drawing to a close, I had to leave and get some sleep. It was a Saturday night. I had to drive to North Carolina the next day and meet Ray at the hospital there. I made sure Ray was aware of what was going to happen, although it was now almost impossible to tell if anything was sinking in.

I told him slowly and clearly, "Honey, I need to go back to the parsonage and get some rest." I paused to see if he acknowledges this. He nodded in acknowledgment.

"You will be transferred to Duke University Hospital tonight." I paused again and got a nod.

"I will drive to North Carolina in the morning, and I will see you there," I told him and got another a nod.

Good.

I was staying at a hotel for a couple of days when Ray was transferred to Penn State Health Milton S. Hershey Medical Center. I moved to a parsonage, which was located on the property of the Spring Creek Church of the Brethren on Friday. It was run by a nonprofit organization called Love Inc., and the stay was free of charge for anyone who was from out of town, but only those who had a relative admitted into Penn State Health Milton S. Hershey Medical Center. It was the social worker who arranged Ray's transfer to Duke University Hospital that told me about it and got me in touch with the church. I called and got an appointment to see the place. I found that it was a very nice place, and it was close enough to the hospital, just some fifteen minutes away. The place was meant for sharing, but at the time, no one was around so it felt private to me.

After I made sure Ray was aware of his transfer that Saturday evening, I went back to the parsonage and started clearing up my things. I had to get ready for my long drive the next morning. The medical team called me at around ten in the evening, telling me they were an hour early. I thought that was great news! The sooner he was transferred, the better. After that phone call, I immediately sent RJ a text message and told him that the flight was an hour early. He already agreed to meet his father beforehand. I suddenly felt tired. Everything that took place over the last couple of days had started to take its toll on my body.

Emotionally, I was all right. I was confident that everything was going to turn out fine. I was just really very tired, and so after I received RJ's confirmation that he will be at the hospital an hour early as well to meet his father, I immediately fell asleep when my head hit the pillow. It was the kind of sleep where you feel like you just blinked and you are awake again and feel that no time passed at all, and it was already time to leave. That is what happened to me, but I had awakened because RJ called me to say that his father was at Duke already. It was 2:00 a.m., and although I was tried, I could not go back to sleep.

I decided to get ready and left at five in the morning, which meant I will be arriving at Duke University Hospital around eleven if I did not make any stops. I stopped once for gas and just followed the now familiar route to North Carolina. It had been a while since I had driven alone long distance. Ray had always been around for long drives. I found myself missing him then. I missed him filling up the silence with his usual chatter.

I turned the radio up and sang along for a little while.

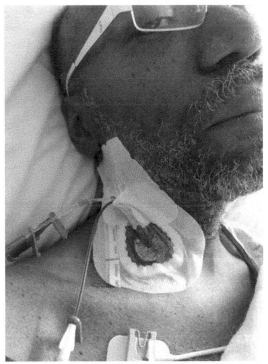

117

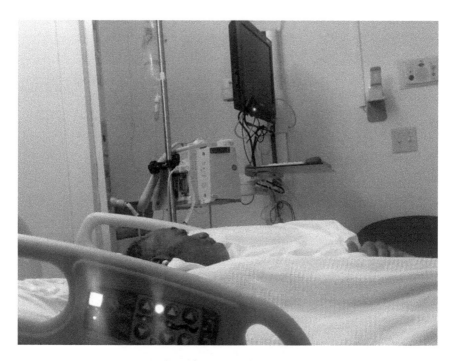

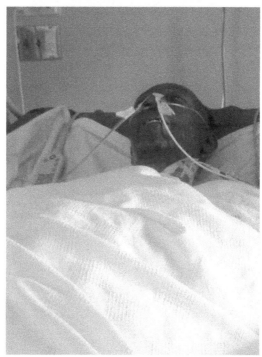

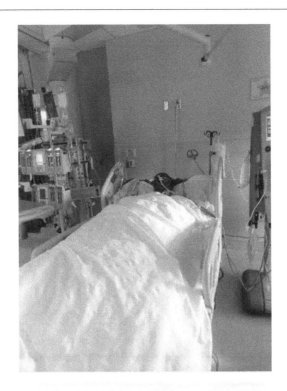

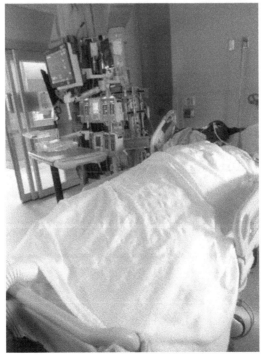

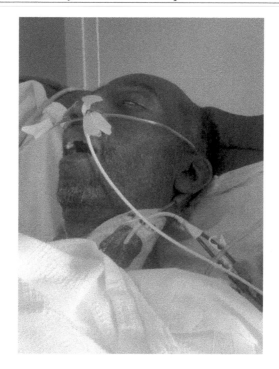

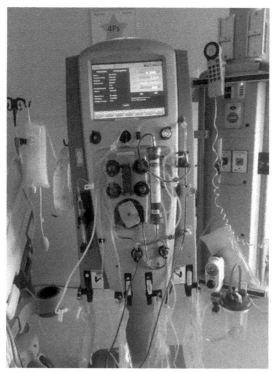

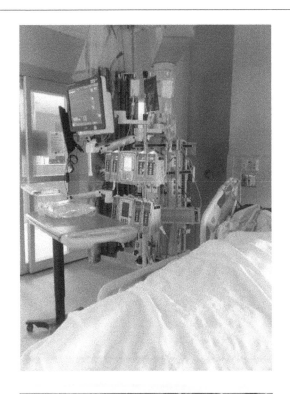

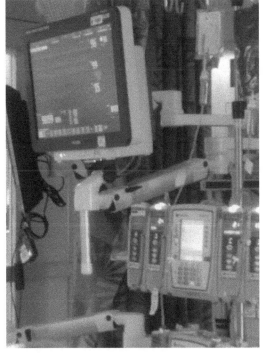

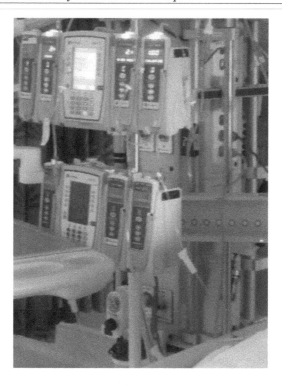

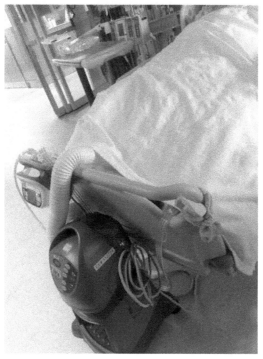

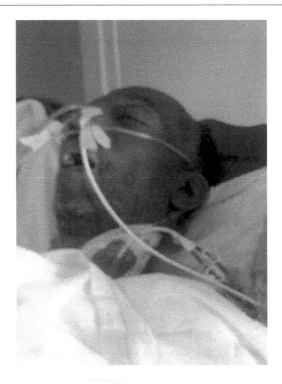

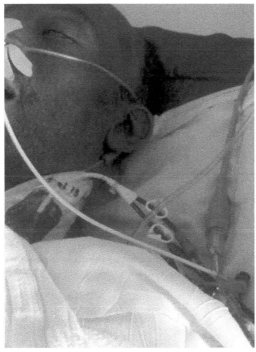

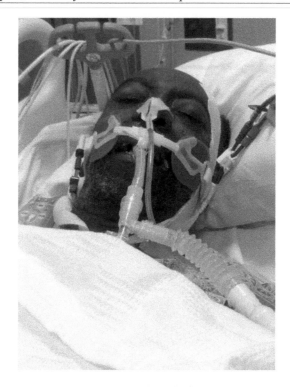

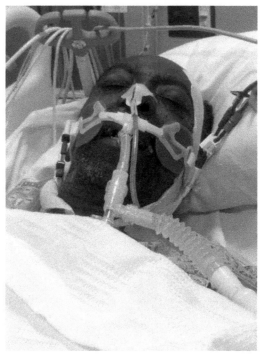

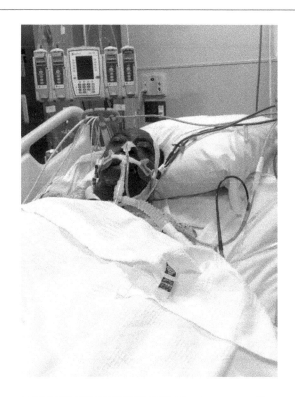

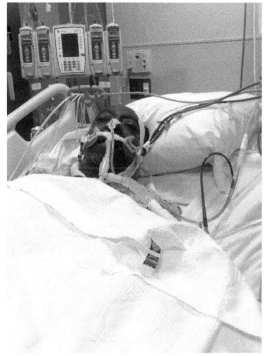

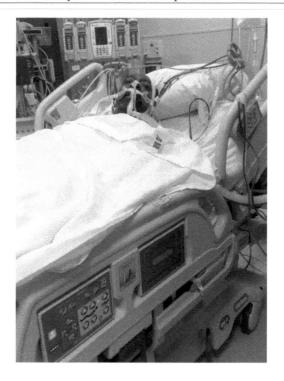

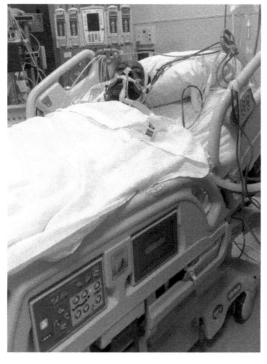

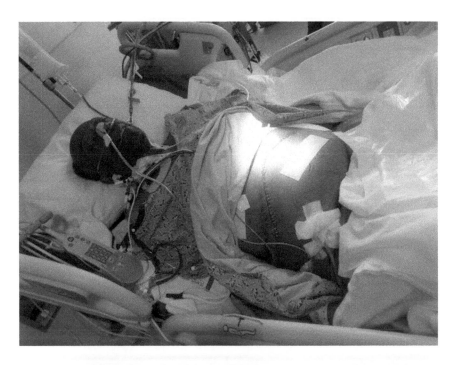

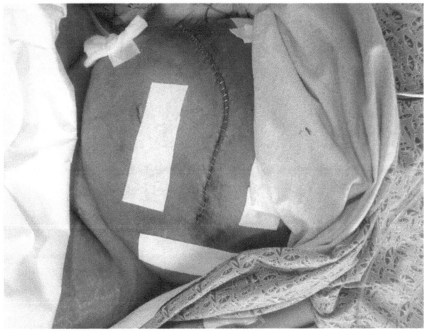

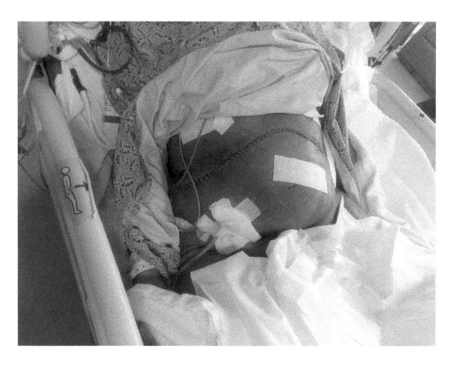

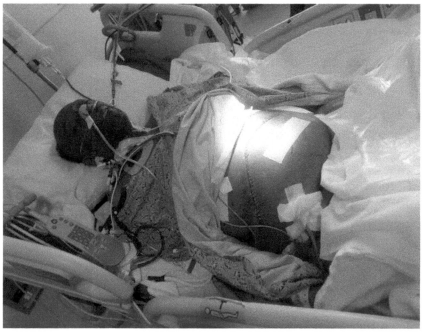

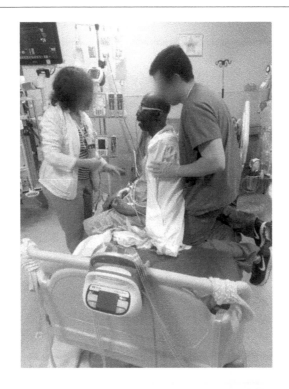

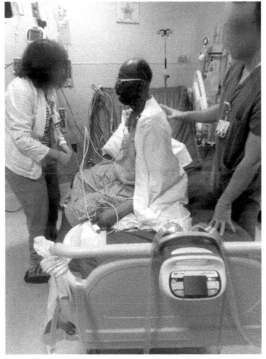

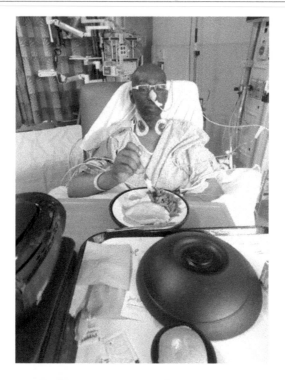

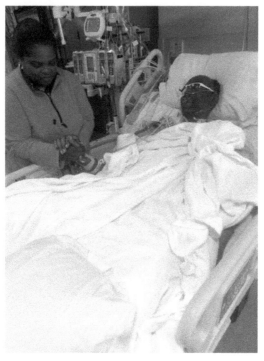

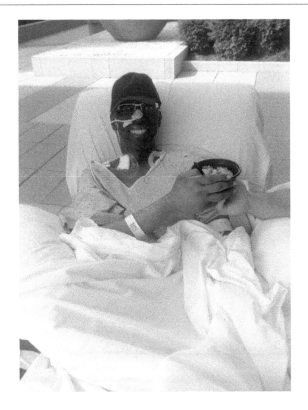

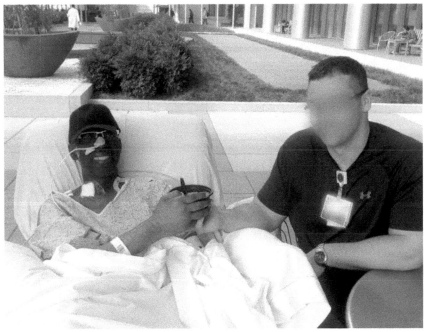

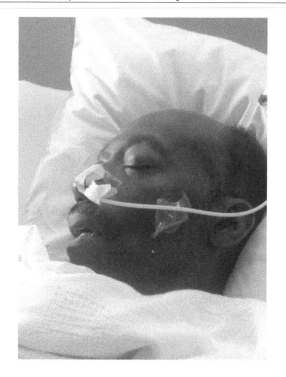

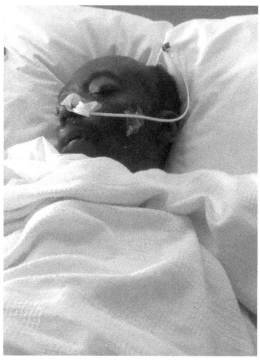

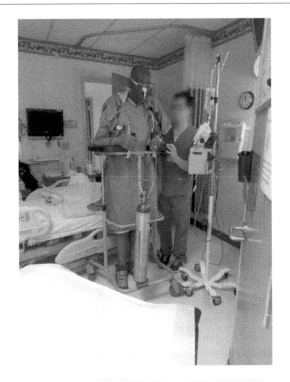

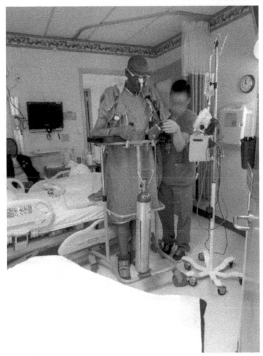

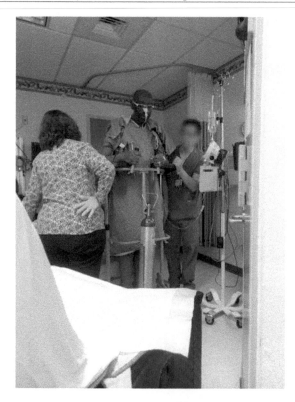

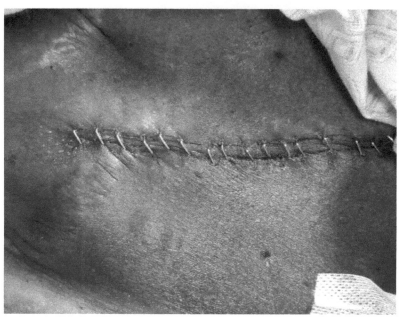

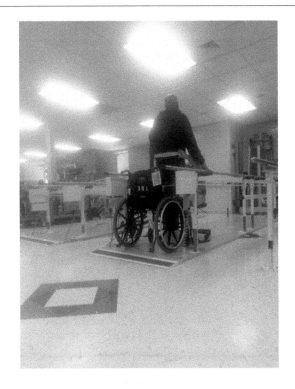

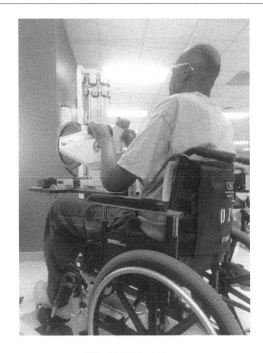

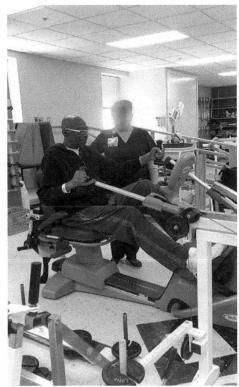

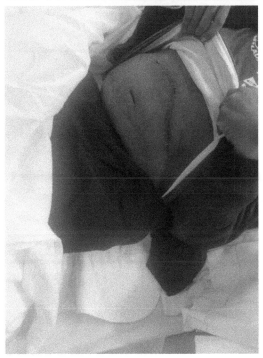

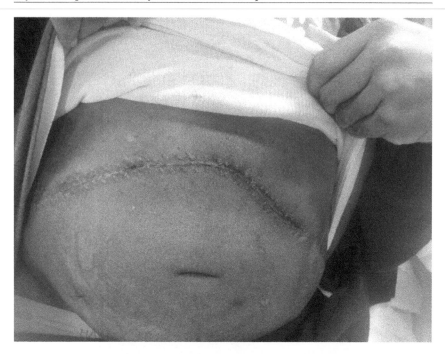

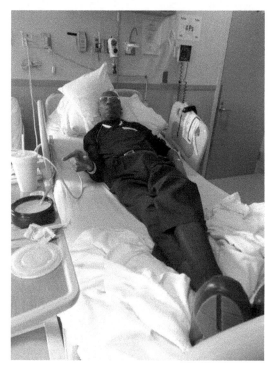

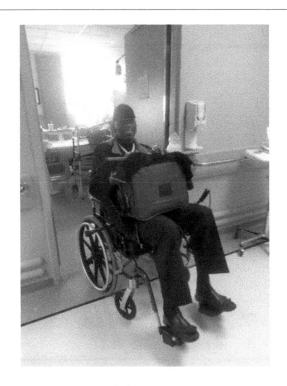

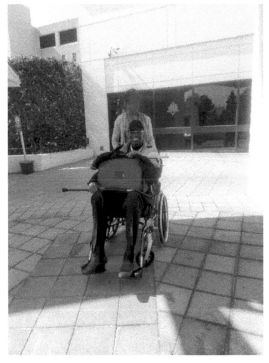

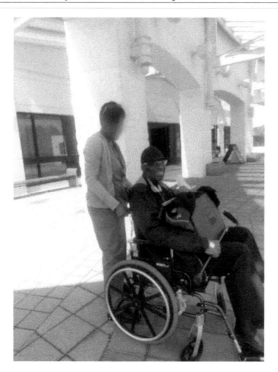

CHAPTER 10

NORTH CAROLINA

Ray

Soren Kierkgaard, a famous Danish philosopher, theologian, and poet, once wrote, "Life is not a problem to be solved, but a reality to be experienced."

By the looks of things, this guy has not experienced the problems and increasing complications of liver failure. I have never pegged myself as a guy that comes and ruins a good joke about how sad his life is, but really, am I supposed to be happy right now?

This is my reality.

Everything is but a two-dimensional portrait of various moving ceilings that are outside of my control. I have been lying down on the same gurney for what seems to feel like an eternity. The long stretch of time and road was made even longer by an assault of mundane memories that just makes me miss doing the things that I had full control over.

I miss the small aches of my body that appear as I wake up in a body that has recently begun its journey to its autumn years. How the weighty buzz of wakefulness invading my head seem to usher a new day and the need for a cup of coffee. Coffee, I miss my coffee. That was how I started off my mornings, but not today.

Today is a much different scenario. Today, it is another hospital, another set of doctors and nurses, same white-paneled ceiling. Today, I am at Duke University Hospital, not unconscious, not unaware, at least not for now.

I am here, present, but I am exhausted. This is the third hospital that I have been transferred to.

I have already been diagnosed with cirrhosis of the liver, and I have a 50 percent chance of survival. That is pretty good, considering. I know this because I remember being told I need a liver transplant. My medical team also checked with me if I knew the reason for this trip.

Well, I knew.

RJ is waiting for me as I arrive. I am guessing he is here because everyone is worried that I might have another episode, and it might be difficult if I did not recognize anyone. I understand that. I am guessing his mother sent him. I am glad to see him here.

"Hey, Dad? How's it going?" he greets me with a smile as he looks at my IV lines.

Was that supposed to be a pun, son? I grin at him. "Hanging by a thread."

As much as I would like to take care of everything, it is simply not possible. I have somehow learned to accept that over the last few weeks. All the paperwork was already done before my arrival, and as soon as Duke University Hospital's medical team received me, everything starts becoming a very organized blur.

Nurses and doctors, one after the other, checking, poking, talking among themselves. A doctor stands over me and begins to ask me a series of questions. I try to focus and answer them to the best of my ability. RJ, thankfully, is helping me to answer them, helping with some sort of paperwork as well.

I hear some of their conversation, but at this point, I am really very exhausted. I have not slept since before my flight, and I do not want to have to think about anything anymore. I want to drown everything out.

It is 2:00 a.m. in the morning on a Sunday. (It is also Super Bowl Sunday.) I make a mental note to thank these people for being here at this time of night. Still at it, still saving lives, still trying to save mine, regardless of the hour. As they rush around and go about their tasks, I am stuck in this bed, helpless, being poked and prodded.

I try to close my eyes, keep them closed. I will fall asleep eventually.

It is suddenly morning. I am not sure whether I was asleep, but somehow I missed RJ. He must have left already; he is nowhere to be found. I am talking to a few nurses, asking about my family, but they are not here.

Where are they?

Finally, it is LyRae who comes in. She holds my hand. "How are you feeling? I got here as soon as I could," she says. "I am here now."

Somehow, she is suddenly talking to a middle-aged woman, a woman who looked to be in her fifties. I drift in and out so much. People seem to be appearing and disappearing at random times. I never know how much time passed every time I wake up. She walks over to my bed and introduces herself as Cristina Sung, and she states that she is my liver transplant coordinator. She is about five foot seven, maybe of Korean descent, and appears to be older than she looks. She had jet-black hair tied into a bun.

Cristina says, "I need to ask the both of you, do you want a liver transplant?"

Responding to that question, both LyRae and I say, "Yes."

Cristina says, "Over the next three days I will be coming to you to explain everything that you will be going through before, during, and after your liver transplant."

And we respond by saying, "Okay."

At this point, Cristina leaves the room.

The next day Cristina comes in and says, "I have studied your records, and you can say that I am quite the expert when it comes to your condition.

"First, there will be a battery of tests you have to go through, to qualify for the transplant list. We also have to make sure to address all other, if any, illnesses. I am in charge of explaining and educating you about everything before, during, and after your transplant, the whole process. I am your person. If you have any questions, I will do my best to answer them. I will come around every day, just as often as your doctors. I will be up to speed on your condition." She says all this in one breath, pauses, and flashes a wide grin.

"Pleasure to meet you," she says as she gently takes my hand in hers. I am not really expecting a response. She is very hard to ignore. Her presence is just magnetic. She is the kind of person who you like instantly upon the first meeting. She came in, and she was larger than life. She is gravitating.

I am going to go through another series of tests, Cristina is saying. As she goes on, I start to drift away again, losing focus. I can still hear her talking faintly in the background.

Sigh, another day of poking, prodding, and blood work. This week's greatest hits.

I just want to get everything over and done with. I cannot complain even if I wanted to.

I should be scared, but I am numb.

Numb with fear?

No.

Numb with something.

Thank you, Doctors. I am numb; but I am aware that a liver transplant should instill terror, fear, panic. I am feeling none of these things, just a numbness that I do not quite understand, a numbness that is consuming me and my ability to feel.

In the next few days they will keep checking the condition of my heart, check for blood diseases, even a dental exam, I heard. I feel nothing, just the same numbness.

Every day, another test.

Every day, I will get much worse.

Everything that they administer and check are necessary to qualify me for the transplant list. That much is clear to me; I need to be on that list.

I need a new liver.

Every other disease or sickness must be ruled out for me to get on that list. I want to say that I am in pain. I am not. I do not feel anything. "This will sting a little," a phlebotomist would say just before taking my blood. I see them poking around me with their needles, but the sting never comes.

I used to try and remember the faces and names of my nurses and doctors. There have been so many, and my awareness has been declining quite rapidly, gone more often than not. I have decided to stop trying. Different faces, different purposes coming in and out of my room. I find it is impossible to keep track of them all. I have learned to just trust in their system.

They want to do a stress test now. I do not know what this is supposed to be, and so I have no idea what it will be like.

"It is medically induced," the doctor says. "This is to check how much your heart can endure."

He injects something that makes my heart race fast like I am running a marathon. I understand that it is induced, but it kind of messes up your perception. My heart is racing, but I am just lying down, not doing anything. It is very taxing, but my heart and I apparently pass it.

I cannot keep track of everything that goes on around me. Sometimes I do not know how much time passes before I am doing yet another test. Like now, they are about to give me an MRI scan.

"This is a noninvasive, safe, and painless scan," the radiologist is saying.

I wish I could respond, but I cannot. I am too exhausted. I have not really slept since I left Penn State Health Milton S. Hershey Medical Center in Hershey, Pennsylvania. I look at her, and I wonder if she knows that I am here, that I understand, that behind what I am assuming is a rather empty look that I am giving her, I am aware.

"Blink once if you are ready for this." I blink once.

"Good!" she says.

Two nurses lift me up and onto the bed. They are saying something about the mirror where I can see everyone when I am in there.

"Be as still as you possibly can," they are telling me.

"The loud noises you hear is just the camera taking pictures to tell us what is going on in your body." I blink once to confirm that I understood.

My bed moves up and in toward the machine until half my body is inside, and it stops. A loud rhythmic banging sound starts. I close my eyes. I can hear my heartbeat in my eardrums. No matter how much they prepare you for this, an MRI is scary the first time around, even the second. This large tube encapsulates you and makes loud banging, clicking noises.

They said that they give earphones to children and play music to drown out the sound of the machine, that I could get one too. I passed on that. The sound seems to grow louder and louder with every passing moment, and just before I start feeling claustrophobic, it stops as suddenly as it started and my bed moves out.

I find that LyRae is standing just next to the machine, waiting for me. I did not even realize she was here. Somehow my brain did not acknowledge her presence until this moment. Maybe it was the absurd amount of information from the transplant coordinator, the stress test, then the MRI, I do not know. Everything is jumbled up in my head.

I feel a pang of emotion gnawing through the numbness. It is guilt, gratitude, and relief all at the same time. Guilt, for having to put her through this, for even thinking for a second that I was alone in this. Gratitude, I cannot even begin to imagine how I could have gone through with this without her help. Relief, to know that I am not alone, to know that she will always be there, my constant.

She holds my hand. "Everything okay?"

Two words, just two words, and the numbness, the bitterness, melts away. A flood of emotions break through me. I want to cry, laugh, and scream in pain all at once.

They start taking me back to my room, and LyRae is taking charge. She took charge of answering all the questions. I feel a wave of relief wash over me as I watch her talking to the doctors, nodding her head occasionally, and finally, I get my sleep.

I am lost in my thoughts, in my own world, in my darkness; and out of the blue, I hear a question. "Do you trust God?" I open my eyes to see it is LyRae. She is about to head home for the night. "Yes," I manage to say to her.

"Keep breathing and I will see you in the morning," she tells me.

CHAPTER 11

TRANSPLANT LIST

Since I arrived at Duke University Hospital, everything has been foggy. It has been a series of blurs, one exam after another, one doctor after another. Every time I come to and try to remember recent events, I only remember snippets. I vaguely recall my cousin Danny visiting. I am not sure whether I imagined him or not because I do not remember anything else. I just remember him coming into my room, saying hi, asking how everything was. I do not know when he left or if he was some sort of vision. I must ask LyRae.

On the morning of February 11, the doctor enters my room, followed by his team.

"Good morning, Mr. and Mrs. Thompson!" he starts. "There has been progress, Mr. Thompson. You have qualified for the transplant list."

What was that? Am I on the transplant list? I wonder how long it has been since I got here. I am on the transplant list already.

LyRae comes to my side. "Did you hear that, honey? You are on the transplant list!" She turns to face the doctor. "Is there anything we need to do?"

"We will take it from here. All you have to do is sit tight and wait."

I look at LyRae, and I am touched to see how considerably happy she looks after hearing this news. I have been taking each day as it was. Until now I have not gotten a chance to think about what comes next. I was in denial, and I was scared. In denial about how sick I was, scared I might lose this battle, scared of what comes next.

I look at LyRae again, and she seems so much lighter. Like a weight has lifted off her shoulders. It is the first time I have seen her smile, the first time in weeks. She does not know it, but I am fully aware right now. She cannot know. There is no way to tell her, no way to let her know. I can barely speak. I cannot even eat. They have had to stick a feeding tube down my throat at some point because of my loss of appetite. I have become malnourished, they said. They called it a Dobhoff tube. It is a special kind of nasogastric tube or NGT.

I cannot react to things as much as I want to, so she does not know. She does not know that as she sits in that chair beside my bed that I can see her, turning the pages of that magazine she is reading. What is that anyway? Is that *People* magazine? Is it recent? I wonder if Brad and Angelina ever finalized custody of their children. I wonder if the *Real Housewives of Atlanta* came up with something even more dramatic to do. I wonder what is going on with Victor and Nikki on *Young and the Restless*. I wonder if that is what she is trying to hold her laugh for. I see the corners of her lips lift like she has found something amusing, but not amusing enough to make her open her mouth, crinkle her eyes, tilt her head back, and let that familiar fit of laughter out. It is been so long since I have heard that sound, too long.

"Excuse me, nurse," she had called to someone outside earlier.

A nice-looking young lady comes into my room. "Yes? How can I help?" she asks.

"I noticed that my husband is not taking the fluids he is being given, is this cause for concern?"

The nurse checks the amount of fluid I am rejecting. "This happens sometimes, and it is quite normal," she says.

"All right, thank you," LyRae says politely, but I could tell she is not convinced.

As I am lying in my hospital bed quietly appreciating and thanking God for the presence of my wife, my buddy William shows up with his wife. I hear him explain to LyRae that his youngest daughter was too young to come in and so she was waiting outside in the waiting area with his oldest daughter. They will take turns with his oldest daughter to come in so their youngest daughter is not left alone. I am so happy to see them, happy that they are here. My mood got even better. I have known William since we were children. We basically grew up together. He is talking to me, asking me how I am, while I try to respond as much as I can. It has been very difficult for me to communicate lately, and today is no exception. My state has not changed. I am unable to talk or move as freely as I used to.

She calls a nurse again after a while and shows how much fluid I am rejecting compared to the previous time. It looks like I have been rejecting as much as, if not more, than I have been taking. The nurse realizes that this is abnormal and rushes out to find the head nurse. She puts the information on the computer and flags it so the doctor could see it right away. When the doctor sees this, he orders an X-ray and a portable one is delivered to my room shortly after that.

While William is here, the medical team orders an X-ray for me. LyRae found that I had not been retaining any of the fluid I was being given through the feeding tube. She started meticulously measuring how much fluid I have been throwing up since they put it in. She was measuring it all the time, determined to see if something else was wrong, worried that something else was wrong.

The doctor reads my X-ray results and finds that the feeding tube was inserted incorrectly. I am taller than the average person, and they inserted a regular-sized tube inside me that fell short and ended up curling in my stomach, which I could not tolerate.

I wonder how many more incidents I have to go through before the doctors realize that they have to be extra careful with me.

First, they hit a muscle during my paracentesis.

Now my feeding tube is the wrong size.

Granted, these things happened in different hospitals. How unlucky can one person be? I now have zero control over anything in my body. I can only open and close my eyes. I can barely even speak. It takes all I have, all the energy I can afford to use, to even say hi to my wife; but I manage to, every day. I have to. That is the only thing I can do for her at this point.

Before my thoughts start to veer toward and linger on the negative, William and his family say good-bye to me and leave. I see LyRae leave with them. It feels like a while before LyRae comes back into the room.

While she was away I had been wondering what the number 45 meant. It is not my age, is it? No. They cannot have gotten my age wrong.

When LyRae finally comes back, I ask the question that had been on my mind since she left.

"What is that number on the board?"

"That is your MELD score, honey," she says.

I think about that, but I am unsure what it means. I want to ask her what it means, but I cannot bring myself to it. I am just so tired.

"Do you trust God?" she asks.

I respond, "Yes."

"Keep breathing and I will see you in the morning."

CHAPTER 12

COMPLICATION

*E*arly Sunday morning, when the doctors did their rounds, the chief doctor for liver transplants told LyRae that there was a possible liver. LyRae did not get excited because she was aware of things that could go wrong in between hearing about a possible liver and receiving the liver transplant. Therefore, LyRae remained calmed. She thanked the doctors for the information, and they left.

All the doctors I have met and sort of met during my unawareness since I have been admitted to the hospital were always confident, always sure of themselves and what they are saying. Today, one of the younger doctors comes in. He looks like he wants to tell us something. He hangs around by the door before coming in.

Is he checking to see if I am awake?

Is he checking to see if LyRae is awake?

This cannot bode well.

He takes a deep breath and opens the door to my room and comes in. LyRae, as she always does when a doctor comes in, stands up, expectant.

"Mr. and Mrs. Thompson, I am deeply sorry to inform you that there has been a complication," the doctor tells us.

A complication from what? What happened?

"The fluid we took out yesterday came back with results of an infection. We are going to have to decline the liver.

"The thing is," he continues, "because of that infection, Mr. Thompson has been taken off the transplant list, and he will have to be on antibiotics for about forty-eight to seventy-two hours before going back on the transplant list." I can see this young doctor holding his breath, waiting for LyRae's reaction.

LyRae walks over to the doctor, puts her hand on his shoulder, and with more conviction than I have ever seen her have, she says, "It is okay, Doctor. He is going back on that list, I know it, and there is going to be another liver for him."

The doctor, I think, looks touched by this much conviction. I can almost see his eyes watering. "Yes, I am sure there will be," he responds.

"You just have to believe it," LyRae tells him.

As if nothing even happened, LyRae walks back to her chair and sits down. "Do we need to run more tests? What can we do?" she asks.

I admire her for her belief, her faith, and her conviction. She truly believes, with every fiber of her being, that I will survive this, that I will get the liver I need. That child, the one who deserves this liver, will be getting it. He or she will live a long and healthy life. He or she will encounter challenges, pain, and heartache. He or she will love. He or she will work. He or she will make a great contribution to the world. It is God's will that I do not get this liver. Another person needed it more. Another person had a whole life to live, and He was not about to let that person go through life without experiencing things that he or she is supposed to, what he or she is supposed to become. This experience will make that person a better human being. He or she will be kinder because of this second chance. He or she was made to do good, to make a difference in this world. I am happy for that person, whoever that may be.

There must be a reason for all of this. LyRae believes that. I should believe that too.

I was on the transplant list, and it seems I did not get the liver they wanted me to get.

What if I do not get a new liver?

What happens to her?

Has she thought about a life without me? I want her to be happy. I want her to never go through any difficulty of any kind. I do not want her to be alone. Say, if I do not ever get a liver. Say, if I actually die.

Has she thought about this?

Has she even considered the possibility?

We got the two-bedroom apartment in Raleigh, and we got it because of that little alcove I wanted to use for a study. What if I am not around to make use of it? At least RJ and Son'Serae are close by. One of them could move in with her. They would never let their mother live all by herself, no.

I have to consider this possibility. I have to make sure that she is going to be fine, that she will never want for anything. I took care of this a while back. I completed my living will. My sickness never really sunk in until this very moment.

I could die.

LyRae could be alone. No one could ever prepare me for that. Her, being alone. I am supposed to be there. Always. What happens when I am not? Son'Serae or RJ will meet the loves of their lives, and maybe even have children along the way. I might never get to meet my grandchildren. I might not be around for their birthdays, weddings, or family reunions, not even for Son'Serae's graduation.

Have I visited all of the places I wanted to?

Was my life as I intended?

Is there anything more for me to do?

I provided for my family as well as I could, and I am proud to say that they have lived a comfortable life.

Is there anything more I could give them?

Anything more I can do for them?

I ponder these questions and start to seriously worry about LyRae. She seems unfazed though, armed and ready to fight whatever comes next. If she could, she would probably win this one for me.

I do not want her to be alone.

CHAPTER 13

ICU

My kidneys failed. My MELD score has now increased from 45 to either 53 or 55. We are far beyond the 40 mark, which is the normal maximum score. The MELD score ranges from 6 to 40—6 being a good liver and 40 being a point that an individual becomes either too sick for surgery or dies.

I do not know what happened or what contributed to it while I was lying in this hospital bed, they just did. Everyone around me sprang into action and started preparations to transfer me to the ICU.

This was the last thing I remember, and seemingly, all of a sudden, I wake up in a different room. LyRae is nowhere to be seen.

Where is she?

I do not see her, but I know LyRae should be around here somewhere. She would never let me go without making sure I am where I need to be. Never.

Right now, a nurse is carefully inserting a tube down the side of the base of my neck. I should not be awake or aware for this, yet I am.

I do not feel anything, but I can see that is what she is doing.

I am helpless.

Weak.

Bloated.

Out of breath, for some reason. Like I am jogging.

LyRae is being asked to stay behind the curtain, that the nurse will finish soon. I will be hooked up to a slow-running dialysis that runs 24-7. They might as well chain me to the machine.

I wonder if this is a very serious complication that will ultimately cost me my life.

I fall asleep for I do not know how long. Four hours? Eight hours? Twenty-four hours? I do not know. I wake up to people who are excited about somebody's impending arrival. It is one of my visitors. LyRae did not tell me anything about any other visitors today, or maybe I do not remember. The nurses in my room are all smiles.

"Mr. Thompson, do you know this lady?" a nurse says as she escorts my visitor into my room.

"That is my mama!" I say with as much excitement as I can muster. Given my current state, this probably did not come out with the excitement that I wanted it to.

But everyone laughed. My children and LyRae, they laughed because this was the first time they ever heard me call her mama. I always address her as "Mother." Then it dawns on me. My mother is here. Did she fly all the way from New Jersey to see me? She should not have.

"Let me have a look at you, Ray," she says as she approaches me.

I cannot say much, but I am very happy to see her. I wonder how she is feeling about how I look right now. She must be terrified, but she does not show it, not even a little. My mother is independent, but I worry about her traveling alone. She senses this and attempts to dismiss my worry.

"How was your flight? How was the weather? Any turbulence?" I ask her. My voice is hoarse, scratchy. It did not sound like me.

"It was fine. How are you?" she responds.

That was the end of my worry for her. She was not going to have it. Seeing my mother was a pleasant surprise. She stayed with me for most of the day, catching up with the children and LyRae. The day goes on uneventfully. The doctors and nurses continue to come in and out to check on me.

I always know, or I am always aware, when LyRae arrives in the morning. I know she is about to leave, like she is now, when she asks me, "Do you trust God?"

"Yes."

"Keep breathing and I will see you in the morning."

The next morning I sense that my mother is here again, and she is becoming upset. She is trying to get me to talk, but I cannot. I try but I cannot. I want to tell her I am still here, but I cannot. She starts to cry, while everyone looked on, not knowing what to do, how to comfort her.

To change the atmosphere, LyRae starts playing gospel music. She plays it on her phone right next to me. I recognize the song. It is one of my favorites! I try to sing along, but no words or sound come out of my mouth. I sing along anyway, just mouthing the words.

"He is still in there!" my mother exclaims.

"Yes, he is," LyRae says, smiling.

This is making my mother feel better, and I am glad. I try to do the same thing until I was too tired to continue.

I have been put back on the transplant list. It has officially been forty-eight hours since I have been on antibiotics.

The next day, while the doctors were doing their rounds, they stopped into my room to see me. While in the room they shared with LyRae and my mother that another possible liver had been identified. My mother said, "That is good news," and LyRae agreed.

Here we go.

I am still hanging on. I make it another day.

I brace myself for another letdown, but I do not feel the way I felt when they told us I had a liver coming. I now feel I am really sick. I might actually be dying.

That liver will surely go to me, I say to myself.

I need to survive this. I cannot allow this disease to win. I have to beat it. My wife needs me to beat it, and she is doing everything she can to help. I cannot let her down. Every night that I can remember since I have been admitted to the hospital, LyRae would ask me this question before she leaves for the night, the one she is asking me now.

"Do you trust God?"

Every time she asks me this, I always tell her the same thing. The same thing I tell her now—"Yes."

"Keep breathing and I will see you in the morning," she says just before giving me a peck on the cheek.

CHAPTER 14

THE TRANSPLANT

$\mathcal{I}$t is another day. It is not an ordinary one though. It is the day of my transplant, Thursday, February 16, 2017.

I see that LyRae is talking to a doctor and signing a few documents. I can hear her answering questions about my age, weight, and my fasting time. I hear the doctor tell her that he is going to closely monitor me during the surgery, that he will maintain my medications, manage my breathing, blood pressure and temperature, all the while making sure I do not regain consciousness. I think maybe he might be my anesthesiologist. Whatever he is saying, he is saying it with authority and certainty.

He is a formal-looking fellow, well-built and tall. He stands upright, with an assertive kind of posture, like he was standing at attention. Something about him tells you that he knows what he is doing and he is very capable, probably does not make any mistakes either. He is not going to chip a tooth during my intubation. I am not going to be waking up in the middle of the operation.

He starts switching the monitors they have been using to watch my blood pressure, heart rate, breathing, and oxygen level to something portable. One of my nurses came in to take me off of the dialysis machine. It is really happening. I am going into surgery.

I hear everything. I see everything, but I cannot move. I cannot speak. If they ask me to blink once for yes or something like that again, I do not even know if I will be able to do that. I do not know if I have control over one of the tiniest things in my body, my eyelids.

Based on the conversation I am overhearing, I realize a few moments later that I am finally getting a liver. Apart from my MELD score, another factor to qualify for a new organ is geography. As Cristina Sung explained it at one point, the United States is divided into eleven regions and further divided into multiple donor service areas, otherwise known as DSAs. Organs are procured and allocated for recipients in the same DSA, and this policy was implemented to minimize times for organ transportation and preservation.

At this moment, I am the sickest person needing a liver in North Carolina, South Carolina, Kentucky, Tennessee, and Virginia.

Somehow, the Lord has granted me a second liver. This is somehow yet another miracle.

What were the chances of me getting a match from the transplant list?

What were the chances of me getting a match from the transplant list *twice*?

This was in His plan, I know it. The person who got the first liver was meant to get it, to serve a higher purpose.

I truly believe that this second one is the one for me. I am sure there is also a plan for me, and this is something I have to figure out when I am better.

I start to wonder where it came from, whose liver it was. How that person lived, how the Lord ended his or her life, and somehow gave me a chance to live mine longer. There are three types of organ donors, and I cannot help but wonder what kind of donor I got.

What if my body rejects the liver?

There is always a chance.

There is a 25 to 50 percent chance that my body will reject this liver, and it could happen within the first few weeks post-op. This could happen if my immune system thinks the liver I got is foreign. That happens, doesn't it?

I try to recall some of Cristina's discussions, and I cannot think of anything. Nothing comes to mind, but I remember her. I remember that there were discussions, discussions about rejection.

What happens to me if my body rejects the liver?

Do I go through this entire process again?
Will I not recognize my children again?
Worse, will I not recognize my wife?

The places that my mind is wandering off to are getting a little morbid. I remember Cristina Sung always had a way of explaining things in a good light. Implying serious ramifications, but presenting them in ways that do not come off scary. Best to stop thinking about negative possibilities right now. I have faith that whatever happens after my transplant can be predicted and controlled by constant lab work and follow-ups.

I am getting a good liver. Cristina Sung had said that the family of the donor had a choice to get to know me, to see where the liver was going, to see what kind of person gets to live because of it. They are given a choice to reach out to me, the recipient. If this turns out to be a success, I wonder if I am going to hear from them.

I intend to live out the second chance at life that I have been given better. For one, I will be a stronger person. I have to make a new bucket list with LyRae. As soon as I can, I will make a new bucket list with LyRae. I am getting ahead of myself.

I try to focus on the things happening around me. Cristina Sung did a great job of briefing us about this operation, so I know exactly what was going to happen during. I am extremely grateful for having LyRae with me.

I am about to undergo a major operation, and it is scary.

I cannot let myself acknowledge the fear that I am feeling. I have faith that this will go smoothly.

As I am thinking this, they are wheeling me toward the operating room and we stop. We are already out in the hall and on our way, but they are stopping.

"We cannot go through with the surgery yet," says the doctor who was in my room earlier. He is looking at an open book or some sort of binder in his hands.

I am inclined to panic.

What happened this time?

Is there something else wrong with my test results?

Another infection?

LyRae starts to react, but just before she could, the doctor continues, "We just need Mrs. Thompson's signature to perform the surgery. We will get someone from the liver team to come and explain this consent form to you."

I breathe a sigh of relief.

Well now, if I were feeling better, I would laugh with relief. I am out here in the hall ready and prepped for surgery, waiting. I am not sure how much time passes before the doctor finally shows up to have LyRae affix her signature on the document that gives the hospital permission to do the surgery.

They start to move me again, and as we reach the doors, we stop for a second. I guess this is where I part with my family until I see them again after surgery. LyRae walks over to my side and holds my hand, she tells me, "I will be here waiting for you when you are done. I love you, and we will see you later!" They start pushing me toward the surgical area.

I start to think about everything Cristina Sung told us about this operation. First, they will be opening me up by creating a long incision across my abdomen to access my liver. It is a good thing that I will be completely unaware for this procedure. I cannot imagine somebody cutting me wide open on an operating table. I imagine the sharp blade cutting through my skin, and it frightens me to my very core.

Since I have been on antibiotics to prevent infection, he will go ahead and remove my liver by disconnecting its blood supply and bile ducts and remove my diseased liver. I will be without a liver for a few moments. I forgot to ask Cristina exactly how long this might be. A scrub nurse or the other surgeon will then deliver the donor liver to the table to be placed inside of me. The surgeon will expertly reattach the blood vessels and bile ducts to my new liver, and once blood flow is reestablished, the surgeon will start closing the incision and the transplant is done.

Oh, how simple it all seems.

I am now about to enter the operating room, and I do not know how to feel.

Is it okay for me to be excited about this? That I am finally going to get a new liver and start feeling better?

I have started to look forward to the things I miss doing. I miss the simplest things. I miss eating solids, cutting up my own food. I miss being able to go to the bathroom without assistance. I miss being able to walk around. I miss being able to drive around. I miss going outside and breathing in fresh air. Sometimes I ask LyRae to crack a window open in the middle of the day. I am tired of being so helpless.

I am so close to getting it all back.

I stare at the surgical light head as the surgical team prepares for my surgery. I remember reading some things about this, about the surgical light head. Back in the day, operations could only be done during certain times of the day where they can use natural light and dependent on the weather conditions. Operating rooms were strategically placed in parts of the building that can receive good lighting.

I wonder if the surgeons can see everything they need to see inside my body with that light. What if their hands cover something with their shadow? One of the scrub nurses moves the operating light. I suppose they do this during the operation as well and move it as needed.

There are about six people in the operating room, two surgeons, three scrub nurses, and the anesthesiologist. I am about to go under into a medically induced coma. My anesthesiologist had already given me anesthesia intravenously. The next time I wake, I should be in a hospital bed again.

While the surgery was in process, I remember looking down at the body on the table. I could not determine if it was me on the table or not, but I do remember the team of medical staff in the room. It was as if I was having an out of body experience.

"When is he going to wake up, Doctor? Is it normal for him to be out for this long?" LyRae asks.

"This is normal. As to when he wakes up, that is entirely up to him. We do not wake the patients. We let them wake up on their own," the doctor responds.

"It has been a little over twenty-four hours. Should we be worried?"

"His vitals are normal. All we can do is wait. He will wake up when he is ready to. The anesthesia should have already worn off by now."

I can hear them, all I have to do is wake up.

All I have to do is open my eyes.

The doctor is right; the anesthesia has worn off. I can feel my fingers and my toes. I can move them a little bit.

I wonder if LyRae can see. If she sees, she will be a little less concerned.

I guess it took me longer than it felt to open my eyes because she is no longer in the room as I finally manage to wake up. I still have a breathing tube attached to me.

"Welcome back, Mr. Thompson!" a nurse says to me when she sees that I have awoken.

I want to respond, but I could not. I want to move, but I could not. I start to feel the restraints on my hands.

I have been tied down.

CHAPTER 15

DELIRIUM

"*Hi*, honey!" my wife says as she enters the room with my mother.

I had been awake for some time, but I have been drifting in and out of sleep. It is finally morning, and I get to see my visitors again.

"Hello!" I greet them happily. My voice surprises me. It did not come out as loud as I intended. It was almost a whisper.

"Do you know what happened?" LyRae asks.

"No." I honestly do not know what is going on. Trying to remember anything would give me a small migraine, so I do not bother. I distract myself by observing everything that is around me, without thinking of the why or the how. I look around. I tell myself I am in a hospital room. There is a nurse outside. A laptop on a portable stands by the door that my nurse types something on every time she comes to check on me. The TV is on with the volume down.

"You had a liver transplant on Thursday. That was two days ago. Today is Saturday."

A liver transplant?

No, that cannot be. How could I not know I had a liver transplant?

"Huh?" Is it Saturday? How much time have I lost?

"Are you all right, Ray?" my mother asks.

"Yes. I am just trying to think how I had a liver transplant without knowing it."

165

The morning continues uneventfully until my best friends stop by to visit. Rodney and Glen. They come and pray with me and try to make me laugh. I have known each of them since we were twelve or thirteen years old. We've been best friends for thirty-six plus years. They have always been around for me, and here they are again.

In the afternoon, LyRae and my mother leave my room to go to the waiting area. They tell me I have other visitors. I wonder who it could be, and they are Christopher and Gale. They are from Atlanta. I met Christopher twelve years ago when I was living in Baltimore. Our church had invited an elder from Atlanta to preach. Christopher came with that elder. Christopher was his armor bearer, as I was my own pastor's armor bearer. I was asked to pick them up at the airport. We connected instantly when we met, and we have been best friends ever since. We lived in different states for most of our friendship, but we have kept in touch over the phone throughout the years.

He and his wife are here in my room now.

"Hello, old friend, how are you feeling?" Christopher says to me.

"Hello, Ray, it is Gale. We heard about what happened and wanted to check in on you. Ray, do you know who that is?" Gale asks.

"Christopher, my friend. I want my wife and my mother, is that all right with you?" I ask both Christopher and Gale.

Christopher tries to continue to talk with me, but I say, "I want my wife and my mother."

At that point, Christopher and Gale feel as if I am throwing them out of the room. Christopher feels very bad for being asked to leave the room by me.

"All right, we will be outside." Both Christopher and Gale leave the room and go back out to the waiting room.

A few moments later, LyRae and my daughter Son'Serae come in.

"What are you doing here? I did not send for you, so you can leave. Please get my mother," I tell Son'Serae.

"Ray, did you send Christopher and Gale out? You know, they drove all the way from Atlanta, Georgia to see you. They are not going to be here very long."

I ignore that and say, "I have something important to tell you and Mother." I wait for my mother to come. I want to tell them both something very important. My mother finally comes back to my room.

"Mother, I need you to tell LyRae that you love her. I need you to tell her that she is a good wife to me."

I wait for my mother to say something, but she is just looking at me and then at LyRae, confused.

"Honey," LyRae starts, "I already know. Your mother has told me this, and you know this."

"No. Mother, tell her. Tell her you love her."

"I love you, LyRae. You are a good wife to my son," my mother tells LyRae. With that, I am pleased.

LyRae leaves and goes back out to the waiting area with our children, along with Gale and Christopher. LyRae leaves my mother in the room with me.

Later in the afternoon, I begin talking persistently. It is if I am having a conversation with someone, but those around me are unable to follow the conversation. One conversation involved my son, RJ, and the second conversation involved Billy, my cousin by marriage.

"He has already agreed to it. We talked about it before, and he agreed to it, didn't he?"

"Who has agreed to it?" LyRae asks.

"RJ, RJ has already agreed to it. We talked about it before, and he agreed to it, didn't he?"

"Agreed to what?"

"RJ, RJ has already agreed to it. We talked about it before, and he agreed to it, didn't he?"

I also mention that Billy was a bishop.

The moment I started talking, I found it difficult to stop, even when I was not making any sense. Later that night the doctor decides that I needed to rest, so he prescribes some medication so that I would go to sleep. However, I continued to talk throughout the night.

The next morning I find myself unable to stop talking. I continue to have conversations involving both my son RJ and my cousin Billy. Still, no one around me could understand the conversations. When this conversation began, I was speaking to a shadow and I continued to speak to this shadow. It was my belief that I was speaking to God.

It is later that evening when the doctor says to my wife, "He needs to sleep, so I am going to prescribe something stronger than I prescribed last night."

The medicine prescribed worked, and I fell off to sleep and slept all night.

CHAPTER 16

WAKING UP

I wake up. From what I am told, it is a Monday, four days after my surgery. I was apparently talking a lot about things that did not make any sense to those around me. That it sounded like a one-sided conversation. However, my conversation was with a shadow, which I strongly believe was really God. I try to recall this, but I cannot. When LyRae finally tells me about it, I just laugh.

"Really?" I ask her, amused.

My voice is hoarse and weak but still kind of there. It hurt, so I do not feel I should be talking at all anymore.

"It was a lot of things that we could not follow. It sounded like you were talking to yourself," LyRae says to me. "You kept repeating that you already talked to RJ about it and that RJ agreed. RJ was standing right there! He did not know what 'it' was that you were talking about though. You were saying so many things like you just wanted to talk, so we just let you. You were not talking to any one of us in particular, so eventually we tuned you out." She chuckles. "Do you remember this?"

I shake my head in response.

"Well, I do not think you are supposed to. The doctors are saying that it was completely normal."

The doctors arrive for their usual rounds and ask me how I am feeling.

I feel normal, save for some pain where my incision is, but that should be normal. I do not think it is a big deal.

"Are you feeling any pain?" one of the doctors asks me.

I nod in confirmation.

"Could you point to where the pain is?" he tells me.

I respond with a nod as I pointed to the right side of my abdomen.

He proceeds to check on it and finds fluid building up in my abdomen, where my incision is. At this point, I have staples and they had put a drainage tube in to collect the fluid that accumulates.

The fluid is normal. The amount of it is not. It is starting to pool. I need to go back into surgery so they can add a second tube. The doctor says that they also need to check if everything else is normal, check for any internal bleeding.

I have to go through another surgery.

I come to the same day. I am in the ICU again, and I am pleasantly surprised to find Mom in my room. I am very happy to see her. I enjoyed her company and the rest of my family's company all throughout the week.

It looks like this room may be my home for the next few days. Apart from Mom and LyRae, my mother, my son, and my daughter are here. I think they have been here since my first surgery. My awareness is not only fleeting. It seems to be selective as well. I am glad they are keeping their mother and grandmothers company.

During this week, a physical therapist (PT) and an occupational therapist (OT) would come in every other day to help me move.

"Hello Mr. Thompson, I am here to help you use your muscles again," the PT says with a kind smile.

"Let me know if you are not up for it or if it is too painful so we can stop."

"All righty, but I am feeling good! Let us do this," I tell her.

"Good!" she says as she starts, removing the pillows from under my feet. "I am going to roll you over on your side and get you up to a sitting position." She says this confidently.

I am a little surprised at her confidence. She must lift a lot, or she must not realize how tiny she is compared to me.

"And then we are going to bend your knees so that your legs are hanging on the bedside," she continues. "Are you ready?"

"Yes, just a few concerns. The first, and I do not want you to take offense, I am just curious, do you think we can do this? You and me?" I ask her.

She lets out a tiny chuckle. "Yes, I know we can do this. It will get easier every time we do. Plus, we will have help!" she says as my occupational therapist comes in. "Was there a second concern?" she asks after a short pause.

"Yes. I understand that you are helping me get back on my feet, is there any other reason why we need to do this?"

"There are many reasons, and yes, preparing you for mobilization is one of them. Sitting up will also promote lung expansion, to help you breathe easier. It will strengthen your trunk muscles, and it will become easier to eat."

"Let us do it," I say with determination.

She rolls me over to my side like she said she would and sat me up as she brought my legs to the side of the bed so that they touch the floor. The other therapist is holding me up while she tells me to use my arms to push off from the bed.

I do not like having to be assisted, but I appreciate it. I have been bedridden for weeks, and I feel like a baby. I need to learn to get up all over again.

"Good job, Mr. Thompson! How did that feel?"

"Embarrassing and painful," I say with a small grin.

"No need to be embarrassed. It is quite normal. You should be able to do this by yourself in no time! You are doing very well," she says.

"Thank you very much."

The occupational therapist helps me with my speech, how to project my voice again. She asks me to say hello to everyone in the room. She tells me to say hello to LyRae who is across the room. Simple things like that really helps a lot.

We continue in that fashion, and I am getting better with each day that passes. I am sleeping well. I am cooperating with the therapists. I am interacting and talking more. Tomorrow, I will be cleared to move back to a regular room, which means that I am now more stable. The nurse in the ICU must have felt my need to breathe fresh air that he offers to take me outside. I have not exactly been quiet about feeling a little trapped inside this room.

"You know what, tomorrow I will take you out for some fresh air. Whenever patients get to a point where they can get up, I like to take them outside."

"Thank you! Thank you!" I just feel so happy that he offered. I have not been outside since January 27. It is February 23 now. It has almost been a month. I am very excited.

The next day, just as we are heading out, another nurse informs us that the regular room was ready.

"You know what, I will take you out anyway. There is a food court over at the next hospital. They have got all sorts of food, sandwiches, Chinese food, you name it!" my nurse tells me.

"I think I will go for the Chinese food."

LyRae, RJ, my mother, and I go with the nurse and go out to the food court. There are tables and chairs outside where I wait with the nurse while everyone else got food. As much as I think I want to eat solid food, I only take a few bites. I sit there, grateful, breathing in the fresh air. We stay out until I start to feel cold. It is time to go back inside. I really appreciate the gesture and thank the kind nurse profusely as we head back to my new room. I am going back to Duke University Hospital. The same nurse wheels me over to the connecting building as I look around.

Hello! I am back!

Hello! I have a new liver!

I want to tell the whole world. I am ecstatic!

I am going along an extremely long walkway. I wonder if LyRae has been using it. It is really quite long. Every person we run into, I try to smile and say hello. I can do that now.

The worst is over. It can only get better from here.

CHAPTER 17

POST-OP

LyRae

I arrived at Duke University Hospital at eleven in the morning that Sunday. It was February 5. I thought that was pretty good time. I made it in about six hours. I started making my way to my husband's hospital room. I did not give myself any time to make observations or make eye contact with anyone. I was in a hurry. I was wondering how my husband was doing alone. I knew that my son RJ left a few hours ago. I wondered if he knew or remembered that I was on my way.

The moment I found Ray, he seemed to be preoccupied with whatever has been going on. I wanted to catch up with what I missed, but I had to see if I could talk to him first.

"I got here as soon as I could," I told him. "I am here now." I addressed the doctors and their questions. I listened and took note of all the things Ray needed to do today. I looked at Ray, and I was not sure if he saw me. I wondered if he was in his confusion state again.

"You can sleep now," I told him, and I concentrated on everything the doctor was saying just after Ray finally closes his eyes to sleep.

In my conversations with the doctors, we were asked if we wanted to receive the new liver. There was no question. Ray needed it. I was given a form to sign to this effect. They needed it in order to move forward.

The next day a transplant coordinator came in and introduced herself to us. Cristina Sung informed us that she will be coming in every day, but that in the first three days, she was going to discuss the transplant evaluation process with us, education, and the patient's responsibility before and after the transplant. I thought this was great news. The more information I knew about the process, the better I felt. I would understand what was expected as we went through the entire process. I looked forward to seeing and working with her.

In the course of the next three days, Cristina came in every morning as promised. She had transplant evaluation forms that I had to look at, some patient information for the liver transplant.

She began by explaining the preliminary procedures. She proceeded to discuss information and set our expectations after listing, like the expected waiting period and who or what is in charge of that. She explained the process of United Network for Organ Sharing or UNOS.

UNOS manages the national transplant waiting list and match donors to recipients. While she was discussing their process and policies, I thought that my husband receiving a new liver will be up to them. I trust that God will guide them to bring us the liver we need. There are a number of factors involved in matching organs, but the most important one that I took note of was how sick you are.

She continued to discuss how we cannot travel farther than six hours away from the hospital before the transplant once he is listed. In addition, we are not allowed to turn Ray's phone off. I understand how important this piece of information is, but there was no way I was going to let my husband out of this hospital until he gets his new liver, until he is better, until he returns to his old chatty self.

Confidentiality and insurance were also covered in her discussions. Now that Ray has what they call a pre-existing condition, he will have to declare this upon signing up with any new employer or company.

In her later discussions, she repeated some of the more important things that we should remember. She did an in-depth discussion on organ procurement, the risks of the transplant and what to expect post-op, what to expect after discharge, and other medical risks like organ rejection. She informed us that the surgery could take six to ten hours, depending on the complexity of the surgery and how bad the old liver was. She proceeded to tell us what to expect in the year to follow the transplant, how Ray will need to maintain anti-rejection medication, that lab work will be done regularly to see how well the new liver is doing.

She discussed the different physicians we were going to be meeting, how some of them would just be in for testing and exams, how everything is under a different doctor. For instance, the hepatologist, a specialist in the area of the liver, the gallbladder, and the pancreas, will manage disorders on these body parts. She also discussed the cardiologist, transplant pharmacist, transplant surgeon, social worker, financial coordinator, medical psychologist, dentist, and dietician.

She informed us that the liver transplant team could decide to order more tests whenever they see fit. She told us that there will be a lot more exams to be done in order to qualify for the transplant list. Ray's teeth will be examined to be sure he did not have any cavities or abscesses, anything they can treat prior to qualifying for the transplant list. He needed an MRI, a CT scan, an ultrasound, a stress test, a blood and urine test, an upper and lower GI test (endoscopy and colonoscopy).

There were a lot of words and terminologies used in our discussions that I have never encountered before, but I remembered them, and I learned them. Cristina told us that we will eventually be getting a liver. She kindly reminded us not to get excited about the first one because anything could happen from when we get the liver to when we need to do the transplant.

She discussed little scenarios that could happen and what we should do. For instance, I should never put my phone on silent. Whether I am at church or anywhere else because the hospital could call to tell me that they found a liver or the hospital could call me if there was any progress on Ray's condition. She explained that while Ray is in the hospital they are going to do as much of his tests and exams as they are able to have done, as opposed to being an outpatient where everything needs to be scheduled. So if there was a liver available for Ray, they will do the surgery right away. But of course, there's a process for all this that was also discussed.

During those first three days with Cristina, I had to read a lot of forms and Ray had to sign them for her to confirm what was discussed and to confirm that we understood what was discussed. She was very good at her job, very knowledgeable. She was very patient when I had questions and always gave me clear, succinct answers. I realized I never stopped and thought of her as a person. I did not know if she was married, whether she had children. She seems very warm and caring. I thought maybe she does have some children. She does not talk about herself much, so I do not know too much about her. One thing I would say, though, was that she seemed very sure of herself and the words that she was saying.

Ray did not acknowledge any of the information shared with us. I could not tell if he was listening, but I knew he was awake. Everything was discussed with him there, regardless of his acknowledgment. The only things he acknowledged were things like, his back hurts, can he get out of bed, he is uncomfortable, things like that. Of course, these concerns were addressed. Other than that, he did not really ask or acknowledge anything else.

The whole process that Cristina discussed eventually began.

Different teams of doctors started to come in and introduced themselves. Ray started going through a series of exams, qualifying exams for the transplant among other things, during that first week. He had a stress test first and then an MRI. I found it a little strange that after his MRI, it was like he just saw me. I saw him visibly relax like he went through so much in my absence and felt that he can finally rest that moment he realized I was there. You could see his expression and entire disposition shift drastically.

"Is everything okay?" I asked him.

He looked at me for a long moment, as if contemplating, as if thinking of the right words to say. Maybe he decided against it. Maybe he could not talk. He did not say anything. He simply nodded his head once for okay.

A lot of other exams were done as well. Cristina did not leave anything out. I expected all of them already. What I did not expect was the doctors had to give him a central pick line because his blood had gotten so thin, which meant that they cannot draw blood from his arms anymore, and if they did, he will never stop bleeding. The line went in the side of his neck, and it had three tubes that the doctors used interchangeably to draw blood or administer medicine.

He also got a computed tomography, more commonly known as a CT. It is an X-ray that will show pictures of Ray's liver. It will show us the size and shape of the liver and rule out liver cancer. He also got CTs and chest X-rays done to evaluate the condition of his heart and lungs.

He got a Doppler ultrasound as well. This would help the doctors assess his blood, to show blocked or reduced blood flow. Cristina said that they will be using a little device called a transducer that is passed over the skin of the blood vessel. This sends and receives sound waves that are amplified through a microphone. This procedure would be done bedside. And again, she said that if any additional problems were identified, more tests can be ordered and these problems could be addressed.

His MELD score had been increasing. It was at 45 at one point.

A MELD score (Model for End-Stage Liver Disease) is what the doctors use to keep track of how advanced the liver failure is and to predict survival within a three-month period. The MELD score ranges from 6 to 40, where 6 being a good liver and 40 meaning the patient is either too sick for a transplant or he or she is dead. They can tell through blood tests namely creatinine, bilirubin, and INR. To say that that is bad is an understatement. I had been asking the nurse on the floor every day what his MELD score was, and she would tell me. I asked so often that she started writing it down on a whiteboard on the bathroom door of the hospital room.

Every day, it was a different number.

Every day, it was a little higher.

Every day my husband got a little bit worse.

The rest of the time, when all the exams and checkups were over and done with, I got some downtime and I got some sleep. All throughout I tried to update the rest of the family about the progress of Ray's situation as much as I can. With each passing day, Ray was getting worse but this also meant he was that much closer to getting on the transplant list and getting a new liver.

In the middle of that first week, a Wednesday, Ray's cousin Danny had come to visit. Ray was somewhat interactive when Danny arrived but started to drift off again after several minutes to a place in his mind that I cannot reach. Danny stayed a couple of hours, talking to me until he had to go. It was the first time we met Danny. Ray only spoke to him over the phone. I hope we will be able to meet him again under better circumstances.

A couple of days after Danny's visit, approximately five days from when Ray was transferred to Duke University Hospital, he was hooked up to a feeding tube. It was a Friday. It was nearing the end of his qualifying exams for the transplant list. He was not eating much. He lost his appetite even before he was even admitted to the hospital. It was one of my primary concerns.

He was malnourished.

You cannot go to surgery if you are malnourished, and so the doctors were making sure that he will be good to go once they have the liver. Malnutrition is a risk factor for higher complications and infections.

I was glad that they addressed this when they did. A nurse came in bringing a long tube to be inserted through Ray's nose. She expertly prepares all the things she needs on a table by her side and starts the process.

"Mr. Thompson, I need you to swallow when I ask you to. It will help speed up this process," the nurse instructed, as he nodded in understanding.

As I looked on, Ray followed instructions. When the nurse told him to swallow, he did it, every single time until it was over. Everything seemed to be going very well, no gag reflexes or anything of the sort. He started having fluids fed to him via the feeding tube. This addition made me feel better somehow, knowing that he was at least receiving all the important nutrients his body needed.

"Good job, honey," I said, encouraging him.

The day after they hooked him up to a feeding tube, the doctors came for their rounds and notified us that Ray was qualified for the transplant list, that he is on the list. At last, a bit of good news! I knew it would come. I was hoping it would, and it did.

We got good news, but I also noticed Ray started throwing up the fluids from the feeding tube. I notified a nurse, but I was told it was normal. I paid attention anyway and started to measure exactly how much and how often he was vomiting.

Later that Saturday afternoon, a friend from North Carolina, William, a radiologist paid us a visit. He came with his family. His youngest daughter had to stay in the waiting room because she was not old enough to come in. William is a friend of Ray's from grammar school. They met when they were twelve, and they also went to college together.

While William was there, I had to call a nurse again. I had been measuring the amount of fluid Ray was throwing up. He was rejecting the fluids from the feeding tube that they hooked up the day before, and I had been measuring his rejections since.

I explained to William that I had already shown the nurse from the first shift that day how much he threw up before when I was told that it was quite normal. I have had a suspicion that Ray was not retaining any of the fluid at all. He was throwing up every fifteen minutes. It looked like he was throwing up more than he was taking in the span of an hour. So, when I had another batch to show the nurse, it was already a different nurse. I immediately called it to her attention. It looked like Ray threw up a lot more than before.

The moment the nurse realized it was no longer normal, she encoded the information on the computer and flagged it. The medical staff came in and took an X-ray. William read the X-ray while it was being taken. He told me that the reason why Ray was bringing up food was because the feeding tube was curled up in his stomach.

It took the medical staff about an hour and a half to read the X-ray. The lack of movement with the medical staff disturbed William until he realized that it was a weekend and there were not many doctors on the floor, that the staff was somewhat of a skeleton crew at the time. An hour and a half later, the medical staff came back and told me that the feeding tube had curled up in Ray's stomach, just as William had said. They were going to stop the feedings.

They saw that the feeding tube was inserted incorrectly and the feeding tube was not the correct size. My husband stands at 6'6" feet tall; he should have gotten a longer tube, which he did not. They stopped the feedings, which in turn stopped Ray from throwing up.

Before William left that day, he said good-bye to Ray and then asked to talk to me privately outside. I wondered what he wanted to tell me when I followed him out.

"LyRae, don't you want to take him home?" he asked.

"Take who home? Ray?" I asked, confused. I was not sure what he was getting at.

"Yes, take Ray home so he can be more comfortable." He told me patiently, surely, all the while looking at me intently, as if trying to read my mind.

I do not know what took me so long to understand what he was trying to tell me. Not for one second did I think about taking Ray home, to make him feel more comfortable, before what, before he passes? He did not say this, but what he was saying, certainly implied it.

No.

He was not going anywhere.

He was getting his liver.

I looked at him as intently as he was looking at me, and I tried to convey the same patience as he had shown me. "William, he is staying here until he gets a new liver."

He looked like he was about to say something, decided against, tried again, and hesitated again. Before he could say anything else, I told him, "I know what I am doing, William. I believe he is getting a new liver. He is going to get better. I need you to know that too."

"LyRae, it looks really bad . . .," he said, trailing off.

"I know how it looks, but I am not giving up. I am confident that he will pull through. I trust the system, and most importantly, I trust in God. I am going to leave him in the hospital and exercise my faith."

He took another long look at me and said, "All right, whatever you want to do I will support you. Know that I am around if you need me."

I knew he meant it. He had already offered to unpack our things. He knew that we had just arrived. He and his wife and children were on their way to our apartment to unpack.

"Thank you, William."

As I watched them leave, I tried to understand why he told me what he did. That was his medical opinion. He thought I should take my husband home, make him comfortable, and wait for him to pass.

Not a chance.

I go back to the room to be with Ray. I learned that they did not take the feeding tube out though. I found out later on that they were still going to use it to give him oral medication. I was just glad that I was able to catch it before anything happened because of it.

I looked at Ray, and he asked me, "What is that number on the board?"

He was talking about the number 45 written on the board of the bathroom door.

"That is your MELD score, honey," I told him. I waited for a follow-up question, but he never asked.

It was seven thirty in the evening, time for me to go home. "Do you trust God?" I asked Ray.

He said yes.

"Keep breathing and I will see you in the morning."

The next day William had called me. It was the day after his visit. He called to apologize. "I prayed about it. The Lord put it in my heart to apologize for the things I said to you yesterday."

"It is all right, William, I understand," I told him.

"I had my doctor's hat on. I should have had my faith hat on," he continued. "I was just so medically focused. How are you holding up over there?"

"It is going more or less the same, still waiting for progress."

"You and Ray will be in my prayers."

"Thank you, William."

I was already back in the hospital when I received William's phone call. The doctors came in bright and early that day to tell us that they think they found a possible liver. I knew I was not supposed to get excited, but I was still hopeful and happy about the news. It was progress.

Duke University Hospital is a teaching hospital. The doctors always came in with a team. There was an attending doctor and a team of residents. They came back an hour or two later, the resident took the lead.

"Mr. and Mrs. Thompson, I am deeply sorry to inform you that there has been a complication," he told us.

He was a young doctor. At the time, I was not sure if we have met him before. It did not seem like it, though. I could tell he had bad news to deliver. I suppose he was having trouble formulating his sentences, how best to say it.

"The fluid we took out yesterday came back with results of an infection. We are going to have to decline the liver and take him off the transplant list and start him on antibiotics.

"The thing is," he continued, "because of that infection, Mr. Thompson has been taken off the transplant list. We had to let the liver go."

I saw him physically holding his breath, waiting for a reaction.

What reaction did he expect? What usual reactions do doctors get?

Outrage?

Despair?

I was not feeling any of that.

Every time a doctor came in, I always stood from where I was sitting. I made sure to pay attention to everything they were doing. I walked up to him and put my hand on his shoulder. "It is okay, Doctor. He is going back on that list, I know it, and there is going to be another liver for him," I told him confidently. Then I went back to my chair, to pick up the magazine I was reading before he came in.

Before I went back to my reading, I asked, "Do we need to run more tests? What can we do?"

"No, Mrs. Thompson, everything will go the same way. We will administer antibiotics for a couple of days. After that, he will go back on the list."

I nodded in acknowledgment.

After they discovered the infection, the hospital sent a new team of doctors that started coming in, the infectious team. They made sure to check for infections. They would also be coming in later on, post-surgery. I sat beside Ray. He was extremely quiet. This was normal for him there, in the hospital. I was still not used to it, but I was adjusting.

Everything will be fine.

We were well informed by Cristina. She did tell us not to get too excited, a lot of things could happen. This was one of those things. While I was thinking this, a few nurses came into the room and started preparing him for transfer.

Something was happening to Ray. He was fine just a second ago. What could have possibly changed?

From what I gathered, the nurse had been checking on the catheter periodically and she documented it, kept a record of it on the computer. This record was available to all doctors, and they kept an eye on it. The catheter had been dry for some time. They waited, observed, and the bag was still dry. Ray's kidneys had shutdown. They were not functioning anymore. He needed to go to ICU to go on dialysis.

After making sure there was a room available, they started moving him to the ICU, which was in another building at Duke Medical Pavilion. The entire place is huge. There are two walkways connecting the buildings, one is for patients and medical staff on the upper floor and the other is for visitors such as myself. This was the same walkway I took whenever I needed to get to the cafeteria. In the beginning, it took me about five minutes to get to that other building. As I got used to the distance, I started making it in three minutes or less.

When we finally reached the ICU, where they put him on a slow-running dialysis, it is one that runs for twenty-four hours through a port on the side of his neck. The port had to be in the right vein first.

"Ma'am, we need a sterile environment. I will need you to wait in the waiting room while we insert the port."

She then started taking an ultrasound to see the right spot. She smiled and said, "I will call for you as soon as I am done."

I left to go to the waiting area.

Two hours later, I had not been called back to the ICU. I wondered what was taking so long. Was there a complication? If there was, I should have been called and informed already. I was getting ahead of myself. I went to the receptionist to check, and I was allowed to go back to the ICU. When I got there, the charge nurse was still at it. She did not ask me to leave anymore though. She said I could stay behind the curtain, and I did.

It took her three tries before she successfully got the port in the right spot. It was before her third try when I came back. They started to put yet another tube through his other nostril to suction the liquid food left in his stomach.

A nurse from the kidney department then came in with the dialysis machine and hooked it up to Ray.

I stayed until she finished, and I made sure that Ray was comfortable before I left at my usual seven thirty that evening.

Before I left, I asked Ray the question I always ask him before I go home.

"Do you trust God?"

He said yes as he always did.

I said, "Keep breathing and I will see you in the morning."

The next day, Monday, Ray's mother Elsie arrived. RJ picked her up from the airport and brought her to the hospital. The nurses were excited for Ray. The nurse asked Ray, "Do you know that lady?"

Ray responded and said, "Yes, that is my mama."

The first day of her visit was quite pleasant. Ray was still responsive to her. They were having a pretty normal conversation. Ray seemed to be worried about his mother flying all the way here by herself. He was able to ask her how the flight was, was it turbulent, things like that.

The next day I drove to the hospital with Mom. When we neared Ray's room in the ICU, I stopped to use the hand sanitizer while she went ahead. It was Valentine's Day.

When I walked into the room, Mom was upset. Ray did not respond to her like he did during her first visit. He did not say hello or good morning the way he did when she arrived the first time. She had started crying.

I was determined to change the atmosphere. It really was quite sad to see her so upset. To lighten the mood, I started to play music for Ray like I do sometimes. He usually responds to that. I picked a gospel station from Pandora and let it play. I looked at Ray, and he started to lip sync to the song. Mom took that as a sign that he was still there, still aware of us.

The station I picked on Pandora played "God Provides" by Tamela Mann. When her voice starts to fill the room, Ray starts mouthing the words.

"He'll come through, when the clouds of doubt rain down on you and test everything you thought you knew. Now you can finally see what God can do, for you. So tonight, close your eyes. There's no more need to fight, watch God provide."

I thought that this song was not only on point, it was quite inspiring. This played until the ad on Pandora came up, you know the ones they play in between songs when you do not have the premium? That happened. I thought maybe Ray was enjoying the music, so I said like I always did when an ad played, "There's another commercial! It is oaky, Ray. It will pass soon. It is almost over!"

After that day, I decided to upgrade it to premium so that we did not get any more ads and I could play music continuously for Ray.

I tried to look at Ray's mother objectively. She was a mother looking at her dying son.

He was bloated.

His eyes were yellow.

Over time, his face had gotten very dark. He looked ashen.

He was hooked up to all sorts of medication, all sorts of machines, and she had no idea what they were for.

Of course, she was upset. Regardless of how updated I made sure she was about his progress, seeing him this way must have been awful. It must have been heartbreaking, not just scary. I decided then to tell her about the prophecy and how I believed with all my heart that it was all going to pass.

I asked her to pray with me, to be strong with me. When I left the hospital that night, I asked Ray, "Do you trust God?"

"Yes," he said.

"Keep breathing and I will see you in the morning," I said.

I went home that night, feeling a little drained. I had managed to keep the mood light at the hospital that day, but it also hurt me. I got home and prayed.

"God, I need your help. You said that Ray had to go through this, but now I am starting to hurt. I need you to move now. Amen."

The following day was a new day. I had to move forward, follow my routine. I went to the hospital as I always did.

Cristina Sung passed by, and I introduced her to my mother-in-law.

Cristina had been routinely checking up on Ray. She always made herself available for any questions or concerns I might have. She was up to date on everything that has been happening.

"You know, it is a full moon tonight," she told me conspiratorially after a while.

That was an odd thing to say, I thought. I did not know where she was going with that, but I was curious, I mean, what is with the tone?

"Is it?" I asked.

"Yes," she said again in the same tone.

She saw my confusion and finally explained, "I do not mean to be superstitious, but it is a full moon and accidents abound."

Oh.

I was not sure how to react to that. Was I supposed to be happy about accidents? I shuddered to think about what sorts of accidents can possibly happen for someone to lose his liver so that my husband can get it. I decided to laugh, "Is that what everyone around here thinks?"

She paused for a moment. "I do not know if there is any truth to it. It might be based on historical data though. Based on my observation, in my experience, around the full moon, I hear that a lot of people act strangely, causing more accidents, more crime. Do I know why? No, I do not. It is just an observation. Some people call it a superstition." She grinned at me. "Well, anyway, do you have questions or concerns I can address for you today?"

"Not for now, Cristina. Thank you so much for dropping by."

"See you tomorrow! Try to be extra careful when you go home tonight. You know, just in case. I am keeping my fingers crossed and hope your husband gets a liver."

I chuckled. "We will be careful and thank you."

Later that same morning, a doctor came in and told us that they had a possible liver for my husband.

Yes, finally.

"I am determined to do this surgery because Mr. Thompson really needs this liver," said the surgeon prepared to do the surgery.

"Did you hear that, Ray? You have a liver!" I told him, but I did not get a reaction. Ray was out of it the whole day. He was not acknowledging anyone at all, not me, not his mother, no one.

Cristina later popped her head in, literally, just opened the door and stuck her head in. "I heard the good news!" she said with a wide grin. "You got another liver! That was fast!" She popped out as quickly as she popped in.

She left us in a lighter mood. We all chuckled at that little appearance. She really is something, that Cristina.

The following day, as I arrived at the hospital with Mom, I was informed that Ray was finally getting his transplant done that day. The day finally came. Looking back at it now, it did not take too long. What was that, eleven days ago? At the time though, the days seemed to drag on. The only thing that was keeping me going was my faith. My faith and my family.

The day of the transplant started off with a lot of documentation. I was signing off on a lot of paperwork and answering questions from the doctors. It was the anesthesiologist mostly. He informed me that the surgery was scheduled for three o'clock that afternoon. I remember looking at the time and it was two o'clock.

One more hour, I had thought.

As the surgery drew closer, the doctors started preparing to move him to the surgical unit. They hooked him up to portable machines, to keep him stable and medicated during the short transfer before taking him to the operating room. Ray's nurse had come in to take him off dialysis. She told me that they did not have a portable one, but that she will be in the operating room to hook him back up to the dialysis machine there.

They started moving him out of the ICU unit and toward the operating room. While we were out in the hallway, the anesthesiologist stops to flip through the binder. "Before we go any further, let me just make sure I have all the signatures."

After a few moments, he then said, "We cannot go through with the surgery yet."

I wondered why not. Another delay in the transplant, perhaps?

No. Please, just no, I thought.

I wanted to ask what happened, but before I could, he said, "We just need Mrs. Thompson's signature to perform the surgery. There is a portion that was not signed. We will get someone from the liver team to come and explain this consent form to you."

I let myself breathe a sigh of relief, it was just missing a signature from the paperwork. This can be fixed in no time. We were all standing out in the hallway, waiting. A team of nurses and doctors, a patient, his wife and family—all out in the hallway, waiting.

Ray's bed was pushed to the side by the wall. I looked at him, and he was awake but unresponsive. I do not think anything registered to him at that point, but I talked to him anyway.

"We had to stop because my signature was missing on the form," I told him.

No response.

"I just need to sign that form before your surgery, honey."

No response.

"We are waiting for someone from the liver team to come and explain the form to me before I can sign it."

No response.

He was not even looking at me, did not seem to hear me.

About thirty minutes later, a doctor from the liver team came out to explain and review the form with me and I signed it then. After which, everything proceeded as scheduled. With that delay, I was no longer aware what time the surgery will be starting. I could not scrub in and hold my husband's hand throughout the surgery. I could no longer whisper encouraging words that he might subconsciously hear. We said our goodbyes to him on the ICU floor, which was on the sixth floor.

The doctors gave us a nod and pushed Ray through the doors that lead to the elevators. The surgery was going to be on the third floor. I turned around and started making my way to the third-floor waiting room with my children and Mom. While in the waiting room, I got a notification via text message on my phone to proceed to the front desk of the waiting area. At first, I was a little worried. My first thought was, maybe something went wrong. I shook that thought out of my system and proceeded to the front desk. When I got there, I was told that the surgery started at four thirty.

The process was like that, and it continued throughout the evening. I would get a text message and go to the front desk for the update. They told us that it was going well, no further updates. The surgery took seven plus hours. I stayed until Ray got out. I did not want to miss any of the updates they might have had. My children and Mom waited with me.

Dr. Burkhart came out seven plus hours later. He looked pleased. He told us that the surgery went well, that the doctors were closing him up and that he would be out shortly. The doctors allowed my children, Mom and I to go to the room to see Ray, as they have throughout that past week, simply because they did not believe that he was going to pull through. The doctors believed that he would die during the week, on the way to surgery or while in surgery. However, none of which occurred due to the hand of God being on his life.

We were all very grateful that everything had gone well, that he made it through the surgery. When we went to see him, I did not know what to expect but he looked the same. He was still intubated and looked like he was hooked up to even more things than when he left before the surgery.

My children, Ray's mother, and I went back to see him the next day, hoping that he was awake.

He was not.

"When is he going to wake up, Doctor? Is it normal for him to be out for this long?" I asked Dr. Burkhart, the lead surgeon.

"This is normal. As to when he wakes, that is entirely up to him. We do not wake the patients. We let them wake up on their own," he told me.

"It has been a little over twenty-four hours. Should we be worried?"

"His vitals are normal. All we can do is wait. He will wake up when he is ready to. The anesthesia should have already worn off by now."

He slept the entire day after the surgery, so my children went home early, but I stayed until my usual seven thirty. He was tied down because the doctors did not want him to pull out the breathing tube. They will be taking it out when they are sure he can follow directions. I noticed him gagging a little on his intubation, and I wondered if that meant he was awake.

That following day, a Saturday, before Mom and I entered Ray's room, we were informed that he woke up the night before. When I saw him, they had already taken out his intubation tube.

"Hi, honey!"

"Hello," he said. His was voice soft and hoarse, more so than before his surgery. I asked a doctor about this later and was told it was normal because he was still full of fluid.

"Do you know what happened?" I asked.

"No," he responded.

I was happy to note that he was responsive. "You had a liver transplant on Thursday, that was two days ago. Today, is Saturday."

"Huh?"

"Are you all right, Ray?" Mom asked him.

"Yes. I am just trying to think how I had a liver transplant without knowing it."

Later that morning, Ray's best friends came to visit, Rodney and Glen. At that point in time, only two visitors were allowed in the room at one time. I had to leave every time he had more than one visitor.

I had to leave again that afternoon when Christopher and Gale arrived from Atlanta. I was in the waiting room when they came back out two minutes later.

"He kicked us out," Christopher told me.

"He what?" I said, surprised. Ray should have been very pleased to see them both. They had become such good friends. I really thought they would have spent more time catching up.

"Yes, he asked for you and his mother," Gale said.

"That is so unlike him. I will see what is going on with him," I said and took Son'Serae with me back to the room.

"What are you doing here? I did not send for you, so you can leave. Please get my mother," he told Son'Serae.

She looked at me inquiringly, and I nodded. "Get his mother."

"Ray, did you send Christopher and Gale out? You know, they drove all the way from Atlanta, Georgia to see you. They are not going to be here very long," I told him.

He did not seem to hear this, or he ignored it. "I have something important to tell you and Mother," was all he said.

When Mom came to the room, Ray asked her to tell me that she loves me and that I was a good wife to him. I was confused. There was something wrong there. This already happened, and Ray was quite aware of this. To be bringing it up at that time was strange.

After that, he started talking about things that simply did not make sense, something about our son RJ agreeing to "it." He did not say what "it" was. I decided it was time to ask the doctor about it. I was especially concerned because he did not stop talking anymore. I was sure that it was causing some sort of strain in his throat because his voice was already very hoarse.

"He is in a state of delirium," the doctor said.

"State of delirium? What does that mean? Like his confusion state?" I wondered.

"I guess you can say that it is pretty similar, but they are not at all the same. The causes are different, but perhaps some reactions might be the same. The confusion state that you are referring to when his ammonia levels were high was different. This was the syndrome your husband was experiencing when his ammonia levels were unstable because of the cirrhosis. What he is experiencing now is what we call delirium. It is quite normal for patients who have undergone major surgery."

"I see, all right." I did not know what to expect. I guess I expected him to just be confused again.

He was given melatonin to help him sleep that evening, but it did not seem to have any effect. Ray was still talking but talking a little more quietly. And he was not talking to any of us; he was talking to himself. And he talked all throughout the night and all of the next day. He would not stop. He would not talk to anyone else either. I tried to listen, to see if I could understand what he is saying, but I could not. No one could. At some point during those two days of him being awake from surgery, I realized that he was not talking to himself. He was actually talking to someone, someone only he could hear.

I realized this as I heard him say the words, "An angel went down at a certain season into the pool and troubled the water. Whosoever then first stepped in, after the troubling of the water, was made whole of whatsoever disease he had."

This was a verse from one of the passages that my husband will tell you he will never forget. There are, I think, maybe ten or fourteen verses in that chapter and he can recite it for you if you asked him. I know this because that was the same passage that his former pastor asked him to reflect on before Ray decided to become a minister himself. What we were hearing was just his side of some of his conversations with God. We eventually had to tune him out until he was over his delirium. My children, Mom, and I stayed at the hospital with him; but we basically had to ignore him.

The next day, it was a Sunday, Christopher and Gale came back. They were only in town to see Ray, and they were leaving that day. I told them that Ray was in a state of delirium. They were both worried about him, but I assured them that the doctors said it was normal. They relayed to me what happened while they were in the room with him.

When they entered the room, Ray was having his one-sided conversation. He was not stopping, so Gale tried to interrupt him. Ray had told her to "keep silent." When she tried to interrupt again, Ray had told her that she was controlling and that he knew this because he himself is controlling. Even though Ray did not allow Christopher or Gale to talk, they prayed over him before they left. Ray talked throughout the prayer. He was still talking about RJ, and then he started talking about his cousin Billy.

The doctors had to give Ray stronger medication that evening to help him sleep. He was hyperactive with all the talking. I was told again that the surgery had gone well. There were not any complications during the operation. His delirium lasted for a couple of days. On the third day, Monday, he seemed back to his normal self, just bedridden this time. He was always confused. "Why am I in the hospital?" he would ask me.

"You had a liver transplant, honey," I would tell him.

Later in the day, he would ask again, "Why can't we go home?"

"You just had a liver transplant. You need time to recover from that," I would remind him.

"Oh, so maybe around tomorrow then?"

I shook my head then and said, "You cannot even get up yet."

"Why?" he asked.

It circled back, and I had to constantly remind him about the liver transplant. I patiently answered all his questions about it. It took some time for it to sink in. It had not really sunk in. I think that to him, the whole thing was just so unbelievable.

The liver team came in every day for rounds. That Monday they came in and asked their usual questions. Ray gave his usual answers, except for when he was asked if he was in any pain. He responded in the affirmative. When asked where he pointed to his incision.

One of the doctors then checked on his incision, where he found fluid building up in Ray's abdomen. The fluid was normal. They had put a drainage tube during surgery in anticipation of this fluid. The amount of fluid building up was not normal though. It was too much, and it had started to pool. They noticed that Ray's bed was always wet. They left and came back several hours later.

"We are not sure what is happening," the doctor said to me. "We do not know why there is extra fluid, so we are going to have to go back in and check to see what is going on."

Four days after his liver transplant, he had to go through another surgery.

It was not over yet.

Mom and I were in the room when they took Ray to surgery. Assuming that it was in the same building as the first surgery, Mom and I started to make our way to the surgical unit, the one at Duke Medical Pavilion. She has had two knee surgeries and two hip surgeries, running or even walking that kind of distance was not a very good idea. She can walk on her own just fine, at her own pace, but not great distances and especially not in a hurry.

We started making our way to the third floor of the building as we did during the first surgery. I registered with the receptionist to get updates, as I did the first time. She looked confused for a second when she looked at the records, and after a few moments, she told me that the surgery was in the other building.

I did not know that. I chuckled to myself and told Mom what happened, and so we made our way to the Duke University Hospital. I knew it was going to be a longer walk, so I asked for a wheelchair for Mom this time, and one of the people at reception desk went and got her one. I pushed her toward Duke University Hospital until we got to the waiting area.

When we arrived at the right wing, we were told that the surgery was in progress and we waited until it was over. It was only two hours long, not nearly as long as the transplant. They had cleared the fluid that was pooling and inserted a second drainage tube during surgery and checked for any internal bleeding. There was not any. They also cleared out the fluid that was in there.

All was well again. The end of our stay in this hospital was finally within reach.

Ray had to stay in the ICU a few more days after his second surgery, but he was getting much better. He was already trying to walk, with the assistance of physical and occupational therapists in the hospital. They came in every other day.

Of course, there were never-ending follow-ups from different kinds of doctors. The liver team, the kidney team, and the infectious team. These are teams of four to five different people, and they all stopped by for daily rounds. Ray does not remember most of them, but I think he might have started to, post-op. The infectious team stopped coming in after Wednesday that week. They confirmed that there were not any infections, and they would not be back.

My mommy arrived the same day Ray had his second surgery. RJ had picked her up from the airport and brought her to the hospital. She was already there when Ray woke up. The day after the second surgery, he was more aware and lucid, more interactive. He is joking with his children again, with his mother and mine, and with me. Things felt almost normal, even though we were all stuck in that hospital room. It was not too bad, the ICU unit was very roomy.

Every other day, the therapists came in to get him out of bed. He could not move his legs, so they showed him how he could move his legs. They were getting him to practice so that he could eventually do it on his own. They got him to stand and pivot. Four days in the ICU, and Ray was already doing better, well enough to be moved back into a regular room at Duke University Hospital. He was out of the woods. That is when they transferred him to a regular room. He no longer had problems taking meds orally. He was interacting and talking more. He was stable. The morning before he was to be transferred to a regular room, the nurse offered to take Ray outside. That day was a Friday, the regular room was not available yet. So, the nurse, understanding how Ray was feeling, decided to take him outside.

Another nurse came in then to say that a regular room had become available just as we were heading out. "I am going to take you out anyway," the first nurse told him conspiratorially. "Let us take you out for some food, what do you say? There's a food court over at the next hospital. They have got all sorts of food, sandwiches, Chinese food, you name it!"

"I think I will go for the Chinese food," Ray said.

The nurse took him out using the lounge chair from the room, and I followed, along with Mom and RJ. We went all the way outside and ordered some food, and we just sat there, enjoying the outdoor scene for once. Ray seemed happy to be outside, but he barely ate anything, and when he got really cold sitting out there, we decided to go back inside and proceeded to go to the regular room.

So again, we went back to Duke University Hospital from Duke Medical Pavilion. He no longer needed the kind of care that he was receiving there. In the regular room, it was more or less the same. PTs and OTs came in too.

The worst was over.

Ray just needed time to heal from his surgeries, but everything was successful. We are now moving forward to the healing part of the whole process.

CHAPTER 18

RECOVERY

Ray

$\mathcal{I}$ have been drifting in and out of awareness for the last thirty days, and when I try to recall anything, my memories are hazy at best. I am still hooked up to some medication and to a feeding tube, but I am feeling significantly better. My mind feels much clearer now. The thick cloud that had always veiled my awareness, the same cloud that has been there throughout my entire hospital stay, has finally lifted and disappeared.

My memories are hazy at best; but the new ones, they start to stay, no longer the fleeting, ever elusive little mix of a memory that eats at me. The things that happened to me, I finally remember.

I notice my doctor coming up for his morning rounds. I am guessing he is my doctor because he went directly to my room without hesitation. There's a group of three other doctors right behind him.

"When can I go home, Doctor?" I ask him excitedly, just as he enters my room. I cannot wait to get out of the hospital and start building a life again. I have so much to catch up on. I will be living in a new city. I have some connections to make, don't I? I should start as soon as possible.

He looks at me strangely, as if thinking, *Did not this guy just come out of surgery?* This doctor, he seems to be new to me, but I know he is not.

He is probably the same doctor who has been taking care of me the entire time I have been in North Carolina.

He clears his throat and says, "Let us give it a few more days. We will see how you are doing and figure out how to proceed from there. How does that sound?"

"Reasonable," I tell him.

A few days?

What am I going to do the next few days?

"Good. I am glad you think so. You got a very good liver, and I must say, you are doing quite well," he tells me.

"Thank you, I feel good, Doctor . . ." I trail off as I realize that I did not know his name. I did not know which doctor he was. My guess is, he is my surgeon. I turn to face LyRae for help, but before she could say anything, he says, "Burkhart, it is Dr. Burkhart."

"Thank you, Dr. Burkhart. I am so sorry, I do not remember much before the transplant," I tell him.

"Oh, that is quite all right," he says as he looks at my records on the computer stationed in my room. "It is normal for most of my patients to forget who I am post- surgery."

He seems to be a very soft-spoken person, a man of a few words, or he is just preoccupied with what he was seeing on the computer. As much as I try to recall our previous interactions, I cannot seem to. I am drawing blanks on all things that happened before I was transferred to this room.

"Which reminds me, these are Drs. Stevens, Smith, and Wilson. They all assisted me with your case all throughout," he says and gestures to his team.

"Good morning, Mr. Thompson," they all say in unison. "It is nice to see you doing so well."

"Thank you for all your help," I tell them.

Satisfied with what he read, he says, "Now, everything looks good. Everything is normal." Dr. Burkhart shifts his gaze from the computer that he is now putting back in its place at the side of my bed to me. "Do you have any more questions for us?" he asks.

"Not for now, no."

"You take it easy, Mr. Thompson. We will check in with you again tomorrow."

As he leaves, I realize I am more disappointed than I let on about not being able to go home yet, but I have to move forward and think about my future.

Let us see, what is next here?

What are my choices?

What can I do to accelerate my healing?

"LyRae, honey, didn't Cristina Sung tell us about what happens after surgery?"

"Yes, she did. You remember that?" she asks, a little surprised.

"Only vaguely. I remember that there was a conversation about it, but I do not recall what was said. Will you remind me, please?"

"Well, she did say that it was possible that you will need to go to rehab after the surgery."

I have already been doing some exercises with a PT and an OT. They had already declared that I was good to go to rehab. This was when the social worker came in.

"Hello, Mr. Thompson, I am Michelle. I have been updated on your situation, and I think I might be able to help you," she says with a smile.

"Thank you, Michelle, I'd like to hear what my options are."

"You have two options. Your physical therapist recommends that you go to a nursing home. I have here a list of nursing homes in the area where you can rehabilitate," she says as she hands over a list.

A nursing home.

I do not like the sound of that, a nursing home triggers memories that I have of my father being in a place like that. It reminds me of all the visits I had to make, the good, the bad, the ugly. It reminds me of a person who is sick and getting sicker every day.

I am not sick anymore, or am I?

I refuse to go to a nursing home. I am getting better moving forward. I feel that it would be a step back.

Going to a nursing home feels like taking one step forward, two steps back. Going to a nursing home is not something I am willing to consider. I have not even seen this nursing home, but it is already a no. I do not want to see the big, beautiful building, always marketed as a "peaceful place," an open space with people walking around, enjoying the sun with their children on a big expanse of grass and trees. That is what they want you to see, but that is not what comes to my mind.

No nursing homes.

"I do not think that going to a nursing home would be the best option for me," I tell Michelle. "What is the second option?"

"Your OT actually recommended rehab. There is an intense rehabilitation program at Duke Rehabilitation Institute in Duke Regional Hospital," she says.

"Intense? How intense?" I ask, intimidated by the words "intense rehabilitation program."

"I am not quite sure about the details of the program, but it is going to be three to four hours of rehab a day, for six days a week."

"I want to do the rehabilitation program. How do we go about that?" I ask Michelle.

"I will get in touch with the institute and let you know," she tells me.

As Michelle leaves, my cousin Debra arrives.

"So good of you to come, Debra!" I tell her.

"I am happy to see you, dear cousin," she says as she comes in for a hug.

"Ouch, that hurts!"

"I am so sorry, are you okay?"

I burst out laughing. "I am fine!" I introduce her to my mother, and they start talking about our other cousins.

She leaves shortly after. It was a pleasant visit.

Michelle comes back with updates.

"Mr. Thompson, I spoke to a liaison at Duke Rehabilitation Institute."

"That is great! What did they say?" I ask, excited.

"They looked over your records and your therapist's recommendations. Unfortunately, they do not think you are a good candidate for the program. You are not active enough to qualify for three to four hours a day of intense rehab."

"Thank you for the update, Michelle."

"You are welcome, Mr. Thompson," she replies. She gives LyRae a nod and a quick smile and leaves the room.

I do not want to believe this.

The rehabilitation center turned me down. I understand that it might not look good on paper or on my records, but I know I can handle it.

Unfortunately, intense rehab is not something that I qualify for. They cannot take me with a feeding tube stuck inside me. They cannot take me because I cannot do anything on my own, at least not yet.

I need assistance to sit up.

I need assistance to sit in a chair.

I need assistance to walk to the bathroom.

I even need assistance to eat. There is a feeding tube inside me!

I cannot keep up with the program, they said.

LyRae sees my disappointment, comes to my bedside, and says, "I am sorry, honey. We can always get in touch with them again later when you can do some things on your own."

I do not accept this.

This is just horrible. I have been very cooperative with my therapists. I have been making a lot of progress.

This is terrible.

I cannot let this little bump stop me.

I cannot give up.

I will not give up. I will get into that program.

One day shortly after receiving the terrible news concerning rehab, I had a visitor that I did not expect. It was Pastor Scottie, Pastor Torain's brother. He entered the room, and I perked up. Pastor Scottie told me that he did not know that I was in the hospital here in North Carolina. I told him that I had arrived on February 5. We had a terrific conversation. Before leaving, he prayed with me. After praying with me, he left.

LyRae, being supportive, she tells me that starting on Monday, the twenty-seventh of February, I will be put on a schedule for physical therapy. I quickly agree. I am all for whatever gets me out of here.

I start being more vigilant in my daily routines. I am trying harder. I need to work with my physical and occupational therapists for an extended period of time each day in order to qualify for rehab. The nurses around here are helping me. LyRae is encouraging me to do better every day. I called my former pastor, Pastor Torain, in Baltimore, the very same one who renewed my wedding vows in July 2016. I call him to tell him everything that has happened and how disappointed I am for having been turned down by the rehabilitation center.

As I am talking to him on the phone, my feeding tube continues to bother me. It just feels too itchy and it seemed to be in the way. It just does not feel right or natural. So I pull it out.

Son'Serae sees me and lets out a shriek.

"What are you doing, Dad!" She runs to me and confirms that, yes, I just pulled out my feeding tube.

"Mom! Moooom!" she screams.

Immediately, LyRae gets up from where she is, which was on the floor. She spends so much time in my hospital room that she had to get comfortable and made a little pallet of pillows on the floor.

Alarmed, she gets up. "What happened?" she asks our daughter.

"Daddy pulled out his feeding tube," she says as she points to the tube that is now resting on my chest.

"Traitor," I tell Son'Serae with narrowed eyes. She ratted me out!

"Ray! Why did you do that? Why?" she asks as she buzzes for a nurse. "My husband pulled his feeding tube out. Can you send a nurse in?" she says into the intercom.

A nurse comes in shortly after that, and she sees my feeding tube resting on my chest.

"What happened, Mr. Thompson?" she asks me.

I think about her question for a second, and I say, "I do not know what happened". The feeding tube just felt wrong, and without thinking, I pulled it out. "I do not know," I tell her.

"Come on now, did something happen to make you want to do that? You know you need that feeding tube until you get your appetite back," she says.

"Nothing happened. I do not know. It just felt wrong."

"All right then, I hope you understand that we have to put that back in," she says sternly.

"Yes, I understand." I am not excited about this. I cannot remember the first time they had to put the feeding tube in, but I imagine it is not very pleasant.

"Now, it is a weekend. Certain people are assigned and authorized to do certain things around here. The person who can put your feeding tube back in will not be around until Monday."

My wife and daughter are standing on the side looking very angry. "Okay," I respond meekly.

It is Monday, and they are putting the feeding tube back in now through my nostril. Everything is going well until the nurse put something else through my other nostril. I think she said she wants to tie a knot behind it.

"Please stop," I say to her.

"It is only going to be for a few more moments, Mr. Thompson, and then it is over," she tells me.

"No, please. I need you to stop. I cannot go through with this, please!" I beg her.

She sighs. "You have to promise me you are not going to pull the tube out again. I only needed to do this to make sure you cannot pull it out. Now promise me."

"I promise, I promise I will not pull it out again. Please stop."

"All right then. I was able to put in the feeding tube. It should do for now. I really hope you keep your promise, Mr. Thompson."

"I will not pull it out again," I promise her. I have to remember to ask LyRae how many feeding tubes I have been given so far. From what she is told me, they took one out before the surgery and put it back after, and now this.

I was so distracted by my daughter's shrieks and screams that I forgot what I was talking to my former pastor about. We already hung up, but the conversation comes back to me.

He reminded me of a verse in the Bible, from the book of Peter.

"Remember that verse from the book of Peter.

'Beloved, do not be surprised at the fiery ordeal among you, which comes upon you for your testing, as though some strange thing were happening to you; but to the degree that you share the sufferings of Christ, keep on rejoicing, so that also at that revelation of His glory you may rejoice with exultation.' I know that it feels that this does not seem to have an end in sight, but often, we think this because we forgot that God is not only in our present but also in our future. He transcends time, He has a plan for us all.'"

He wanted me to remember that when it feels that the trials never end, God will give us the strength to endure it and get through them. I thank him for reminding me and hang up the phone. He is absolutely right. I can do something about this.

God gave me the strength to endure this; I do not doubt it for a moment.

And so, every morning, I wake up, seven o'clock on the dot for a straight week. I know that a lot of pain is about to come, and it is going to do so for the next few days, but I push on. My goals are bigger than my pain.

LyRae gets the physical therapist, and the PT helps me up, the same way the PT in the ICU did, and moves me to my chair. The PT does this by using an electronic lift that the nurses also know how to use, and they do use it for me sometimes; but it is mostly the PT who uses it and helps me to walk around.

We chat a little bit about how I am feeling, and I am surprised to note that I have not yet asked her what her name is. "Did I forget your name? Have we met before?" I ask her.

"No, Mr. Thompson, I have just recently been assigned to this building. My name is Liz, and I am a physical therapist. Another therapist will be here today. His name is Alex. We will be helping you walk."

"Where is Alex, and have I met him before? I am sorry I have to ask. I was told that I lost a lot of memories from the last thirty days. I am just trying to put pieces back together. I wonder if Alex is one of the pieces?"

"I am sorry, Mr. Thompson, I am not sure. You can ask him yourself. Here he comes."

I am relieved to see that Alex stands at six feet. I was little worried I might be too much for Liz alone to handle. I am glad they sent us two nurses for this.

"Hello, Alex," I greet him.

"Good morning, Mister . . ." He trails off and takes the computer from the side of the bed. "Mr. Thompson. I am so sorry, they assigned me to this case last minute, and I did not get a chance to look at the records, but I know that I am doing some physical therapy with you today."

Well, that at least answers my question. I have never met him before.

"Thank you both for being here. I really want to get better, and I would like to be in rehab as soon as I can. Your assistance means a great deal to me."

"You are welcome, Mr. Thompson," they respond in unison.

From either side of me, each therapist helps me to stand up. The goal today is to walk out the door. *One foot in front of the other*, I tell myself.

They give me what they call a Swedish walker to use.

It has four little wheels, kind of like the wheels used for toy cars for children. It just looks like a shopping cart to me. It is tall enough for me to lean on it with my arms.

"Consciously command your mind to move your right foot first," Alex is saying. He must have seen the look on my face. I can only imagine it was agony that he saw because he continues, "No rush, take your time. Liz and I are here."

I breathe in, breathe out.

Okay, mind, feel my right knee and lift it.

Slowly, consciously, I command my right knee to lift, and it feels rusted, like a guitar that has not been tuned for a while, and I imagine my joints are squeaking. I feel my weight shift to the left, and Liz is on that side. I look at her. She seems to be fine. I might be leaning toward that side more than I care to admit, but I press on. I lift my knee and drop my foot a few inches forward and lean to the right, shifting my weight to that side now.

The challenge here is shifting weight to the right side and pulling my left leg and moving it forward.

I try to ignore the pain.

The sooner I do this, the sooner it is over. I put more weight on Alex and try to lift my left leg and move it forward.

"I cannot do it!" I exclaim in pain.

"Yes, yes, you can," Liz tells me. "It is a matter of your will, Mr. Thompson. Do you want to reach the door or not? Because if you do not want to, we can sit down again."

She taunts me.

She brings back memories of varsity basketball. Liz would make a fine coach.

"I want to. I will," I say, determined to reach my goal. It is just a few steps to the door. It is not that far. I can do this.

"Yes, you will!" Alex encourages me. "Do not worry, you can lean on me as much as you want to, just put that other leg forward. You can do it, Mr. Thompson. I know you can."

My body, it is aching. I cannot use my abdominal muscles at all. My incision has not healed yet. I try to put more weight on Alex as I lift my left leg and try to put it in front of me.

All I accomplished is falling on him. He catches me and says, "Good job. Believing in yourself is half the battle. Are you ready to try again?"

I look up at the distance from my bed to the hospital door. It is maybe about five more steps. Five more steps of agony, and while every bone, every joint in my body is screaming in pain, I say, "Yes, I am."

Alex smiles. "All right, let us take one more step."

"Oh, just one?" I manage to joke.

"One at a time," he says as he chuckles.

"All right," I say almost to myself.

Breathe in, breathe out. I am acknowledging my pain, waiting until it passes, bracing myself for a new round.

Bracing for I do not know how many days like this. Bracing for more pain.

Bracing for more failures, but anticipating success.

I make it to my hospital door, and from there, Alex and Liz bring me back to bed. I am exhausted. That was a lot of action.

I am exhausted, but I am also happy.

Today, I walked to my hospital door. That is a lot of progress from yesterday, which was, I sat in a chair.

The end feels closer.

I just have to get into that rehabilitation program. Every day for the next week, Alex and Liz will be helping me to get up and walk until I can get used to being active and moving daily. Until then, I will remain in this hospital, far from the care that I need to get my body to function fully again.

One week of the same thing, but every day I am improving.

Today, the eighth of March, I am walking around the whole hospital floor!

I am ecstatic!

I feel good!

Of course, I am using a walker with the assistance of my PT, and LyRae is walking just behind me with a rolling lounge chair, far enough for me to be confident that I am walking by myself, but close enough to provide assistance.

I am smiling at everyone. I cannot remember their names, but I try to say hi to everyone that makes eye contact. Most of the hospital staff already know me, and I feel like a rock star walking down the halls.

The doctor who is walking and looking at some chart looks up and sees me and says, "Hello, Mr. Thompson! Looking good! Keep it up."

"Thank you, I will," I respond. I continue walking.

The elderly nurse at the nurse's station looks up from her computer and says, "Hello, Mr. Thompson. You are doing great!"

"Thank you so much!" I am almost back to my room now.

Another doctor, bringing back a patient from somewhere, says, "Hello, Mr. Thompson. Did you just do the whole floor and back?"

"Yes, I did," I respond happily.

"Good job! Really, that is amazing."

"Thank you." It is hard not to heal when everyone around you has a positive energy. It is contagious.

I say hi to the nice lady in the next room. She has been visiting the room next to mine for just a couple of days. She is the cutest little thing.

"Good morning, Mr. Thompson! You seem extra happy today. Where are your friends?"

She does not see Alex is right behind me. I cannot help smiling a lot. It is like there is a hanger stuck in my mouth. "That is right I am, missy. I can walk by myself again," I reply happily.

She does not see that LyRae is with me. She is with me all the time.

I make my way back to my hospital room, where I sit at the foot of my bed and start brushing my teeth and washing my face using the portable sink the hospital provided.

A representative from the rehabilitation institute comes in and surprises me.

"Hello there!"

"Good day, Mr. Thompson," she says formally. She comes in and sits in one of the chairs in my room to observe me.

I am surprised that she arrived, but I am also happy to show her how much progress I have made in the past week. I did my stretches and exercises with Alex and Liz, the same way I have been doing all week.

The representative thanks me for letting her see the progress I have made and leaves. "I just read your file a few days ago! And now you are doing all of that! You are doing good," she says as she leaves.

"Thank you, ma'am."

That was quick, I think.

Michelle comes in a little bit later, all smiles. "I do not know what you said or did, Mr. Thompson, but whatever it was, you somehow convinced the representative from the rehabilitation institute that you could make it through the intense program!" she exclaims.

"I did?" I ask, surprised.

"Yes! You are in!" she tells me.

This is the best news. I am going to be discharged from the hospital and admitted to rehab the same day. Michelle did her magic, and everything was arranged. I find myself once again in an ambulance.

This time, though, it is nothing as urgent as my previous trips, nothing life-threatening. I am going to Duke Rehabilitation Institute.

I finally get to do it.

See, when you set your mind to something, follow through, the rest falls into place. I did some rehab in the hospital until I could do things on my own until I qualified for a more intensive program. It took me about a week and a half of pushing myself to my own limits, creating new ones and the pushing for that too.

It is March 8 now. It has been twenty days since my liver transplant.

They took out my feeding tube today, just before they sent me off to rehab. No more Dobhoff tube, no more sticking things down my throat.

The first day of the rest of my life officially starts today. What I am going to accomplish in rehab will prepare me for the real world again. I am like a baby right now. I have to learn everything again—learn how to walk up a flight of stairs, learn how to open a car door and get in. I will get all these normal functions back. I will learn them here, under the care of experts.

I spent all of my first day in rehab resting. I had quite the morning.

The next day I meet my two therapists, a physical therapist and an occupational therapist. By the end of my intense program, I should be independent, I should be able to understand my body again and know when I need to take a break, know my limits.

My physical therapist will address concerns about my posture changes due to breathing patterns, flexibility impairments, skeletal muscle weakness, endurance changes in my muscles, endurance changes in activity. My occupational therapist will develop, recover, or maintain daily living and work skills. This will include exercises on organizational skills as well as speech therapy.

I am not sure how long I will be here. I was told that I can stay as long as I need to until I am ready to go home. Every day I will wake up and start physical therapy. They will be training me for all kinds of things. What exactly? I do not know yet. They did say it was going to be intense back when I was still in the hospital. So I am expecting intense therapy.

LyRae comes every single day without fail. She is here first thing in the morning before I begin my therapy sessions; sometimes she stays the whole day. During one particular visit, she yelled at me because I started picking at the staples from my surgery. They had started to look like scabs, and they were a little itchy, so I picked at them.

"Ray, will you stop doing that!" LyRae says.

The next day I waited for my physical therapist. He should be here any moment now. I wonder what is on my agenda today.

I start to recall meeting him for the first time. It was the day after I arrived at the institute. A man had walked into my room. He is tall, maybe about six feet. He seems to have a very colorful personality. There's a certain air of grace to him as he walks. Everything about him is neat and clean. His hair is perfectly quaffed.

"Good morning, Mr. Thompson, my name is Paul. I am your physical therapist."

"Hello, Paul!" I greet him cheerfully.

"How are you feeling today?" he asks as he brushes the imaginary hair away from his face and tucking it behind his ear.

"I am feeling good! I am very excited to be able to move normally again. What do you have for me today?" I ask him.

"Well, it is your first day at physical therapy. How about we take it easy first, and then we will evaluate what things we can improve on. How does that sound?"

"Sounds perfect!"

"All right, let us begin with some stretching exercises if you could sit up for me please."

And so, it begins.

The day after my evaluation with Paul, the PT, the floor doctor comes into my room later in the afternoon. After our brief dialogue, he proceeds to write something on the board in my room. He writes March 29.

"What is that date?" I ask him immediately.

He looks at me and says, "That is your discharge date."

"That is a nice date, but that is not my discharge date."

With strange, confused expression on his face, he asks me, "What do you mean it is not your discharge date? Your two therapists, me and the other medical team members have already discussed it."

"No. My discharge date is on March 24."

"Well, only you can decide that, but we think your discharge date is March 29."

This is but one more motivator for me to work harder. There is a date to aim for now, a date to beat. One of the assistants at the gym would come in every evening without fail and post my routine for the next day on the board in my room. He is the same assistant who straightens things out at the gym, wipe the tables down, and sanitize after use. I would go over the list and mentally prepare myself for it. I had to be in therapy three to four hours a day, every day except Sundays.

During this first week, Paul had to push me to the gym in a wheelchair. The gym is on the same floor as my room but on the opposite side. I was pushed in a wheelchair until I could walk all the way.

I am tasked to do different kinds of exercises. Paul would make me do walking exercises. There was a block that I had to step up on and step off of. There were handrails on each side that I can use to stabilize myself as I step on and step off. When Paul asks me to do ten steps, I would do fifteen. I would have other walking exercises, such as walking between cones with a walker, walk around the gym in circles. Paul always takes notes on how far I walk and how fast. There was a built-in bicycle in the gym too. When Paul asks me to go five minutes on it, I would do ten minutes.

I had to learn how to walk upstairs all over again. This particular exercise is important because, upon my return to my new home in Brier Creek, I'd have to climb up twenty steps of stairs before I am able to get into my new apartment. Paul evaluated which of my legs was stronger. It was the right one, so as we went along. I would do some exercises that strengthen the left leg more than the other.

Once again, I begin to complain about my staples. LyRae is still fussing at me for picking at the scabs. The administrator comes to my room to check on me, and LyRae and I are still discussing the staples.

"They are so itchy. When can these staples come out?" I ask the administrator.

"We will schedule someone to come in and take those out. I will put in a request for you."

"Thank you very much!"

A few hours later, a very serious looking man comes into my room. "Hello, sir," he says to me.

"Hello there! How are you?"

He stands there awkwardly for some reason. "I am here to remove your staples," he says.

"Oh, all right. It is about time, isn't it?"

"I will check. Will you lift up your shirt, please?"

I lift up my shirt so he can see.

"Yes, it is about time."

He takes a stapler remover looking thing from his bag. I realize, as he was about to remove the staples, that I do not know if this will hurt. As I think about it more, removing staples from my body, I think it might hurt. So just before the staple remover makes contact with my skin, I stop him.

"Wait! Is this going to hurt?"

"A little bit. It is just a little sting."

"Go for it," I tell him.

He inserts the jaw of the staple remover below one of the staples, parallel with my incision. He then squeezes the two parts of the handle together, and the legs of my staples spring open and disengage from my skin. He repeats this process about twenty-nine more times, slowly and surely removing the staples across my abdominal region. Before I know it, it was over.

"Looks like they are all out!" he says, satisfied with how well it went. "How does that feel?"

"Feels good! Thanks so much for your help!" I tell him. It is such a relief to finally have those things out.

"No problem." He takes his things and goes.

You would think that there might be drainage or bleeding after that, but there was none. My incision had already healed.

My occupational therapist, Jane, gave me my first shower after I got my staples removed. They did not want to get the staples wet, so the shower came right after they were removed. I had not had a shower since January 27. Until that point in time, I had only been getting sponge baths. She worked with me on how to wash myself, how to put my shoes and socks on, how to get in and out of the bathroom without falling, basically things that one does as one goes about their day.

This includes getting in and out of a car. They have a makeshift vehicle in the gym that we would use. I get in it, close the door. Open the door, get back out. I would also practice getting in and out of bed, and this would be really hard for me. It requires a lot of abdominal muscles, but I always push on, always do more than what is asked of me. I learn how to move around in the kitchen, how to maneuver to get closer to things so I do not have to stretch too much. Jane would also practice some mental, organizational skills with me. She would make me stand and do puzzles on a table.

I also had a speech therapist for a time. My memory and organizational skills would be put to the test. The speech therapist had to gauge how quickly I can remember things. I did well. I did memory tests with her. I had to answer situational problems, both verbal and mathematical problems.

Of course, my days in rehab were not all therapy. I got a chance to meet the most wonderful people. My nursing aide, Sandy, is my favorite. My relationship with her was similar to the kind of relationship that I have with Son'Serae, always bickering, always joking. She comes into the room, and I would ask her, "What are you doing here? Why are you bothering me?"

She would laugh and say, "I am in your room because I need to do something, but if you do not want me here, I can leave."

She would come in to take my vitals, blood sugar, or other things like that. She was always welcome, of course. On some days, she would be assigned to another area and someone else comes in to take my vitals. I would always ask for her, and she always came.

She would say, "I should get back to my assigned area. You are always distracting me!"

One day, I am not sure if she is a social worker, but she was not an aide or a therapist, but she had come to my room, and we got to talking about God. My situation, her situation, we just ended up talking about it and other things. After our conversation, right before she turns to leave, she says, "You know, I can tell you are a pastor. I feel like I have been in church here in your room, thank you."

Since then, nurses would gather in my room to talk about church or the goodness of the Lord, to talk about anything under the sun, really. There would be three to five of them in my room with me. "What are you all doing here? Don't you all have work to do?" I would joke. They would all laugh. Yes, they did have work to do, but they had time to stick around for a bit, just to talk with me some more. My room was always crowded, but I did not mind it at all. Everyone is such a pleasure to talk to.

Another nurse's aide came into my room offering to shave my face. I was a little surprised and touched by the offer. "That is just what I do. I will shave anyone on this floor," she had told me.

"Go for it!" I said to her happily.

During my last week in rehab, Paul comes into my room with a grave look on his face. "Mr. Thompson, I have news." He broke out into a grin. He could not keep the solemn look going for long. He was happy with me. "You surpassed everything we thought you could do. We agree with you, your discharge date is now March 24."

"Yes. That is right, it is. Didn't I tell you?" I tell him happily.

"You sure did," Paul says as he erases March 29 from the board and replaces it with March 24.

Rehab was going really well for me, until one day, LyRae had gotten a phone call. It was Pop, her father. Her expression had changed from smiling to solemn in five seconds. Her grandmother just passed. I remember we went to visit her in New Jersey before I ended up in the hospital. We drove there. I could not get out of the car. It was during the time I had trouble functioning. So LyRae went in to see her grandmother by herself. When she came back to me, she had told me that her grandmother was not doing well. She was sick. She had dementia. She was now bedridden, and her organs were starting to fail. LyRae knew she was not going to be around very long. We had been praying for her ever since.

The funeral was set for March 25, and I was distraught. I had known her for over thirty years. I really feel like I should be there, but I was not allowed to travel.

"But I am getting out the day before. I can make it there!" I told LyRae.

"You cannot travel, honey. Remember? You are not allowed yet."

"I am going to ask my doctors."

"You can do that, but you are really not supposed to travel."

I asked my doctors, and as always, LyRae was right. They did not let me attend the funeral. I was very upset I could not go, but I told LyRae that she should go.

"If you want me to go, you will have to stay in rehab until I come back."

"What? No!" I said, angry.

There would be no one around to care for me at home. I would be left alone. Although I was making good progress in rehab, I was not quite ready to be home by myself. I was angry, but I agreed. She should not miss her grandmother's funeral.

Talking to Pop during that week, I expressed my regret for not being able to go. He had told me that I could make a video to be played at the service. I thought that was a good idea, and so LyRae had to bring me a suit and tie that I would put on for my video. Wearing sweatpants (which I hated, but that was all I had in the room) would have been inappropriate. My name was included on the program. When LyRae returned from the funeral, she told me that people thought I was around after they saw my name in the program. But I was not there, of course. Everyone else realized this after my video played.

"Hi, everybody."

Everybody said hi back during this brief pause, as per LyRae.

I said the following in the video, "I too will miss Grandmom. She was a beautiful woman. She had a loving spirit, and I will miss her along with you. I am eager to see the rest of the family again. Let us remember the good times and memories we had with Grandmom."

I signed off after that.

It was after I completed the video I realized how much Grandmom meant to me. It was in my prayer that I thanked God for Mrs. Barbara G. Nelson, a beautiful woman with a beautiful spirit.

On Friday, March 24, LyRae and Son'Serae drove to New Jersey for Grandmom's funeral. I thought that I was going to be alone over the weekend; however, I was surprised by a visit from one of my dearest friends. Regina came to visit me. I met Regina in 1986 as a freshman at Howard University. Over the years our lives had changed so much, but we remained the best of friends. I was so excited to see her. She kept me company every day while LyRae was in New Jersey. Regina stayed the entire weekend and visited with me every day. We talked about all our friends from our days at Howard University, along with our lives in between then and now. Given the fact that she and I both were members in the Church of God in Christ, we talked about our denomination a lot, catching up on stories. I truly enjoyed my visit with Regina, and she left on Monday, the day of my discharge from rehab.

LyRae drove back from New Jersey on the twenty-sixth of March, and before I know it, it is March 27. My stay in rehab was such an amazing time, and I am grateful to have met everyone there.

As much as I enjoyed my time in rehab, I am very excited that I am going home today. Duke just released me. A nurse's aide pushes me in a wheelchair toward the elevators and to the front of the building with LyRae walking with us. We wait out front for LyRae as she left to get the car. I cannot help smiling and thinking about the last time I was outside.

I was given a day pass the weekend before. A day pass allows you to go outside of the facility for a few hours. I was excited then, but not as excited as I am now. During my day outside, LyRae took me out for a drive. We drove by our new apartment. As we pulled in, I saw the familiar brick building with ivory siding. It has three floors, and our apartment was on the second floor. It has a balcony and a very long deck that you can see from the outside. As we drove by, I saw Son'Serae standing there, waving.

"That looks a lot like our daughter, LyRae," I said with a grin.

"It is our daughter. I told her we would drive by before we left," she said to me as we both waved back.

The drive was an interesting experience. It made my heart happy to get a glimpse of my new home, but the drive was excruciating. Every little bump on the road sent shockwaves of pain throughout my body. I told myself that it was only temporary, that it will not always hurt that way. Of course, that did not make anything less painful. I was determined to enjoy my day pass. LyRae thought it was a good idea to just park somewhere, and I agreed completely.

We drove to Duke Botanical Gardens, where we parked and sat in the car for a while. My white cell count was low. I did not think it would be good for me to be around people; it will be very easy for me to catch something.

"Don't you want to go out and walk around?" LyRae asked.

"Not today. Let us just sit here for a bit and enjoy this view," I told her.

We sat in comfortable silence. I really liked my view, the change of scenery. The green of the leaves, the yellow of the flowers, children playing—all were a refreshing sight to see. I tried not to think about how long it has been since I saw anything like that. I was simply thankful that I was outside once again.

We stayed for about half an hour to forty-five minutes, and we had to head back to the institute. It was time to go back to reality. I comforted myself with the thought of going home soon. It was not going to be that long, and here I am now a week later, ready to go home.

I am going home today. I am going home to my new apartment in Brier Creek. I am sleeping in my own bed tonight.

I hear two honks, and I see LyRae's car pull up. I smile to myself. My occupational therapist practiced with me to get in and out of the car. She was a sweet woman, Jane. Always patient, always encouraging. She gossiped a little too much, but it was so much fun.

I proudly stand from the wheelchair and got into the car while the nurse's aide waited until I was safely in. I thank her and say to LyRae happily, "I am ready!"

"We have to stop by the clinic first. We have to meet the pharmacist, your new liver coordinator, and Dr. Burkhart."

Oh right. I knew that.

"Let us do it!" I tell her.

We meet the pharmacist to confirm that I had all my medication in order, to make sure that we knew how to read the chart for my medication. I also meet with Teresa, my new liver coordinator, for the first time. The thought reminded me of Cristina and how helpful she was. Our meeting with Dr. Burkhart went well. He says that my progress is impressive. I am very pleased with how well I am doing and how everything is going, but I really just want to go home.

Dr. Burkhart makes sure to remind me to always put on sunblock because I am at risk for nonmelanoma skin cancer or NMSC. Apparently, skin cancers are very common after a transplant, and I will be regularly examined for any type of skin cancer. He advises getting a dermatologist as soon as possible so that the dermatologist can be familiar with my condition now and be alerted if there are any slight changes.

Other than my appetite and the NMSC, the pain medication was not working, or at least I have been in a lot of pain over the last week and I do not think it was working. Dr. Burkhart gives us another prescription for a different kind of pain medication. Since this clinic prioritized patients in the hospital first over outpatients, we have to wait a bit.

LyRae and I decide to grab something to eat. We get a cheese pizza each.

I used to love cheese pizza.

I cannot even finish mine. I struggle to eat at least half, and that was it for me. We finally get my medication from the pharmacy and head home.

On the drive home I contemplate the next three months again. I will set an earlier goal. If I work hard, if I do not slack off on my therapy, my diet, I am sure the doctors can clear me for work sooner than three months.

My apartment is about twenty minutes away. I am finally heading home. I am sitting in the passenger's seat of a car, not in an ambulance on the way to yet another hospital. I am going home. I sigh contentedly.

"You excited to go home, hon?" LyRae asks while driving.

"You bet I am."

I am enjoying my view, enjoying all the simple things that I have been missing during my hospital stay. I appreciate every stop, every turn, every tree that we pass by. Even the pain that I feel as the car hits a bump, I can appreciate that because I know that I am going home.

"Can we roll the windows down, please?" I ask.

"Of course," LyRae rolls down the windows and immediately the cold air fills the car. It is a nice day out. I close my eyes and breathe it all in. It feels good to be out again. This is good.

"Everything all right, honey?" LyRae asks. She is always worried now whenever I go long periods without speaking. In the hospital, it had meant I was out of it again and going through another bout of hepatic encephalopathy, that my ammonia levels were high again. All that is behind us now.

"I am just enjoying the fresh air, the wonderful view. There are no words to describe how happy I am to be going home."

"We are here!" she happily announces.

RJ and Son'Serae are waiting outside for us.

RJ opens the car door and extends his hand. "Thank you, son, but I want to try and do things myself." I might have spoken too soon because I now see the twenty steps that I have to go up, the ones I have to climb.

"Okay, I take that back. I need your help," I tell him as he laughs.

"Mom, you can take his right side," he tells his mother.

One step after another.

I tentatively take my first step.

Right foot first, here we go.

I feel my abdominal muscles strain. I feel the pain where my incision is. My skin stretches and pulls.

It hurts.

I let out a soft grunt.

"You okay, Dad? You want to take a break?" RJ asks me.

"Of course not. I trained for this for weeks! I can do it!" I tell him defensively.

"All right, all right. Take your time, just let us know if you want to stop," he says.

Second step, here we go.

It is the same process, over and over. The skin around my incision stretches and pulls.

Did I really have a liver transplant? That cannot be.

I go all the way up to the twentieth step and stop to rest.

I did it!

I look back down and smile.

I should celebrate.

I practiced for this. The actual thing is actually quite different, but I did it. *I did it.*

"Do we have any alcohol to celebrate my victories?" I say jokingly.

LyRae and RJ look at each other and start laughing.

"Okay, Dad, slow down," RJ says.

Slow down.

The worst is over, but there are still so many things to keep in mind. I am glad and I feel extremely lucky that LyRae has this all down. I doubt very much that I will ever be able to keep track of everything by myself.

I put a real effort into trying, though. LyRae, my angel, has it all under control. I still have several appointments with Doctor Riley this year. I have to go and see him once a week and will continue to do so depending on my condition and recovery.

Every appointment will be a few hours long as I will need to get some lab work done every time. This is important because we will have to look out for any indication of complications. This is a risk for all transplant patients. I have to be religious about my appointments and blood work, on top of my medications.

Apart from my medications, I have to keep a close watch on my temperature. I need to check it once a day and notify my doctor if it is ever greater than 100.5. I am to check my weight daily and notify my doctor if there is any sudden weight gain. I am to check my blood pressure twice daily. I am going to need to incorporate all this into my routine. It is only going to be tough the first few days, but I should be fine.

My next goal is to try and get rid of this cane as soon as possible. I do not like needing it. I try to do simple exercises at home, the ones that I have been taught in physical therapy. I think of all the other things that I have to keep close attention to that I should be calling my doctor or be sent to the hospital for: rashes; swelling in my mouth or on my skin; any redness or swelling or drainage from my incision; nausea, vomiting or diarrhea; burning or pain in urination; any headaches, sore throat, changes in my vision, blood in my urine or stool, shortness of breath, any increased swelling in my legs or abdomen.

That is a long list of things that I cannot possibly remember. I walk into my apartment and look around. Yes, I am glad we decided to take this place. I walk over to my new favorite spot, a small alcove that has been converted into a study. I smile as I see a list of things that I should be paying attention to.

I have not yet been declared fit to work yet, but I believe that is going to happen quite soon. My abdominal muscles are still on the weak side, hence the cane. Doctor Burkhart said three months. It has only been about a month since he said that. What am I going to do for two months?

I sit down in my old chair. I am happy LyRae has been able to organize everything at home too. She really is an amazing woman. I wonder if Son'Serae ever got a break from school and came over to help.

I stand back up again, grab my cane, and walk around my apartment. It feels a lot more like home now. I have not gotten a chance to see what LyRae did to our bedroom yet, so I make my way there. I take my time, trying to get used to the place. It is very different from that apartment in York, Pennsylvania, a lot roomier, and I like it. I walk down the hall and make a left.

I open my bedroom door, and I am touched that it looks almost the same as our bedroom at our home in York, Pennsylvania. LyRae got my favorite sheets from storage! She must have prepared this for my arrival today. I have really missed all this. Although this apartment is very much new to me, it already feels like home.

I finally made it home.

CHAPTER 19

GOING HOME

I woke up a little confused.

Where am I?

You know how you wake up in a new place and you do not recognize anything? For a few seconds you do not know exactly how it was you came to be there.

Everything starts coming back, slowly and then all at once.

My mind is an empty beach. Memories start approaching, like a tide coming in.

The first wave pulls and crashes, filling the emptiness of my mind with events from the past.

We thought about moving to Raleigh. We looked at a bunch of different options, and this was the apartment we picked.

Another wave starts, pulling and then crashing.

Our things are in it already. I recognize the dresser, the curtains, the sheets. The bed I am sleeping in is familiar, comfortable.

It feels like heaven. That is right, heaven.

My wife arranged for all of our things to be moved here while I was . . .

Where was I?

I wait for another wave.

It does not come.

I try to get up, but I find it to be extremely painful, particularly in the abdominal region. I lift my shirt up and look at my stomach. There's a long, thick horizontal scar right across my upper abdomen.

I walk over to the closet and open it, just to make sure this is not all in my head. My clothes are in it, all folded neatly. My shoes are arranged neatly on the shelves along with LyRae's.

I am home, finally. It is real.

I make my way to the bathroom. Slowly, surely, I took a shower. LyRae had prepared for my arrival and had put a handicap bench and a handicap commode in the bathroom. What a lifesaver! I cannot stand up straight in the shower yet, the bench helps a lot. As I step out of the shower, I decide to weigh myself. I am 168 pounds now.

After getting dressed I start to make my way out of the master bedroom and into the living room.

Where is everybody?

And as if I conjured them up, they appear. My daughter Son'Serae and my son RJ walk into the living room.

"You are awake, finally!" Son'Serae says exasperatedly.

"Well, good morning to you too, sunshine," I respond sarcastically.

"How are you feeling, Dad?" RJ asks.

"Oh, you know, old," I tell him.

He chuckles. "Do you need anything? Mom says you like to eat before you take any of your medication."

Medication?

"Where is your mother?" I ask.

"Right here, hon!" she calls from the kitchen.

I hear her. She does not sound too far away. I know how close the kitchen is, but the thought of walking over there was an exhausting one. I know I have to do it though. It was now, or I will never do it.

I get up slowly and change my mind.

I am not hungry anyway.

I think I am going to the bedroom instead. I want to lie down again.

"Uuuuh, where are you going?" Son'Serae asks.

I ignore her.

"Daddy, where are you going?"

I did not want to answer. I need to get to bed before anyone can stop me.

She follows me into the bedroom a few moments later and finds me already in bed. She stands over me, hands on her waist.

"Stop being so lazy and get up!" she demands.

I close my eyes.

"Oh, don't you go pretending to be asleep. I know you are awake."

Silence.

"Dad."

I ignore her.

"Daddy!" she yells.

I open my eyes. "Get out," I tell her, and she storms off when I playfully throw a pillow at her, failing to hit my target. It fell short. She turns around to make a face and closed the door. I was not even close.

My aim is off. Everything is off.

I chuckle to myself, thinking of my daughter. It is fun to make her angry sometimes.

LyRae comes in to bring me oatmeal as I did not feel like eating anything, but I eat it anyway. I feel that I need to eat before I take my medication. I need to take about twelve pills and that is just in the morning.

I stay in my room and spend the entire day there. Son'Serae comes in from time to time to nag about me being in bed. I spend the day ignoring her. It is always nice to have her around.

"What are you even doing here, young lady? Don't you have school?" I ask her.

"I told you, Dad, I am staying a couple of days until I move into my apartment," she says to me.

Did she tell me that? I do not remember. My memories are still a little foggy, or maybe just selective.

I honestly do not want to move. RJ comes in too. He is not as aggressive as his sister, but he does drive by the apartment once a week.

I want to rest. It is just so comfortable to be in my own bed again.

I think I fell asleep. I could swear it was dark when I closed my eyes, and it is bright outside again.

I still do not want to get up.

LyRae seems to never be in bed when I wake. She is coming in now. She does not look happy.

"Ray Thompson, you get out of that bed right this instant," she demands.

She was standing over me, all demanding, a very serious look on her face. I burst out laughing. I find it so absolutely adorable.

"All right, all right, I am getting up. I am!"

"Do you need help?" she asks, suddenly concerned.

"It is fine, I got it. I got it."

I don't got it.

"Yes, actually. You know when I need a little help," I admit.

She helps me up and takes me to the kitchen where I eat another bowl of oatmeal and look at all my medication.

I have so many.

It is divided into little sections in this plastic box, divided according to days and times. LyRae had carefully arranged this for me.

Why do I need so much medication?

"You had a liver transplant," LyRae reminds me.

A liver transplant.

I try to walk around with my cane. LyRae comes with me, outside and around the complex. I begin to familiarize myself once again with the surroundings. I am glad we chose this place to move to.

I walk around, maybe less than a block, just up to where the trash cans are, and head back. I run into a couple of people and introduce myself as their new neighbor. They seem to already know LyRae.

This first week that I am home, I am still adjusting. Although I learned everything again in rehab, I find the actual thing is quite different. I suppose my mind is preoccupied with my new surroundings, concentrating on moving my muscles are just a tad bit difficult.

I spend most of my days in bed and walking around a little with no particular schedule and no particular destination. I just try and make sure my muscles do not get rusty, and then I rest again. LyRae is on the phone every day, following up on the physical therapist who is supposed to come in for my home sessions. No one came in all week.

After a week at home, it was time for my first doctor's appointment.

Dr. Burkhart, my surgeon, is happy with my progress. My incision is healing quite well.

"All right, so during your surgery your gallbladder was removed," he tells us.

What.

"Say that again?" I ask him.

"Your gallbladder was removed," he repeats. "We had to remove it because it was too close to the liver. We do not want any gallstones or blood clots that close to the liver. We remove it automatically." He looks at LyRae. "It was in the paperwork."

I look at her too. That is strange. She looks as surprised as I am.

LyRae is silent for a moment and starts to laugh.

"It was probably in the paperwork, but we were standing out there in the hallway, on the way to surgery. I had no time to go over every single item on that thing!" she explains.

"Well, I did not know it was missing . . .," I say.

"The gallbladder is not absolutely necessary for human survival. It is involved in the production, storage, and transportation of bile that breaks up and digests fatty foods. I need you to watch what you eat and avoid the fatty food," he tells me.

"Skip the bacon. Got it," I note.

It is hard to be upset about my gallbladder, hard to miss something you did not know was not even there anymore.

After hearing about the fact that my gallbladder was removed, Teresa went on to say that while reviewing the pathology report, they noticed a small spot in the liver. It was after examining the small spot in the liver, they realized that it was cancer. The doctor had found cancer in my old liver.

However, the cancer had not spread anywhere, to any other locations in the body. After hearing this fact, I looked toward heaven and threw my hands in the air, and I thanked God for preserving me. If that cancer would have spread I would have been diagnosed with cancer of the liver in the future, but all I could say was, "Thank you God for your hand of protection.

"Dr. Burkhart?"

"Yes, Mr. Thompson, what is it?"

I ask him the question that has been on my mind since I first got back home. "When can I go back to work?"

He looks at me strangely, as if I just said something incomprehensible.

After a short pause, he clears his throat. "Let us give it about three months, and you can start looking," he continues. "You just had a major surgery, a liver transplant." He pauses to make sure his last sentence sinks in.

It does not.

I still have trouble grasping the fact that this happened.

"Everything will depend on your progress. Three months is good time. You got a very good liver."

Three months?

I was thinking at most, three weeks.

What am I going to do for three months?

I was so excited to finally live in Raleigh and explore my job opportunities. I am here, but now I have to wait another three months before I can even start looking for a job.

I cannot imagine what to do with myself for the next three months.

As if reading my mind, LyRae says to me, "You can focus on your physical therapy and getting used to your medication, your maintenance."

For three months? I do not know. I try not to show how disappointed I am.

"What about the cane? When can I get rid of it, you think?" I ask him.

"You can get rid of it when you are ready. It is all up to you. When your muscles are stronger, you will find you will not be needing it," he says with a kind smile.

I am going to give myself one more week and see if I can walk without it.

Apart from that, I do not have any other concerns. LyRae, however, is concerned about my appetite. I have only been eating oatmeal; food just was not tempting. I do not know how much Boost Breeze she ordered, but it seemed like an endless supply.

It is a nutritional drink. Boost Breeze mixed with ginger ale, and this was the only thing I did not mind drinking. This was discovered while I was still in the hospital. It was suggested by my dietitian (yes, I had a dietitian).

Once the medication for my appetite kicks in, I should start gaining weight and everything will start falling into place. It takes a couple of days for the medication to kick in, and when it does, I finally start eating two meals a day, eventually, three meals plus snacks.

My physical therapist starts coming in after my first week home.

Two nurses also come to visit that same week. The first nurse is an intake nurse. The second nurse is in charge of taking my vitals and confirming the medication I am on, making sure that I am on track.

I notice there is something strange about that second nurse. I only realize it as she leaves. She seemed a little off. She just was not friendly or maybe she was just spacey. I know she was there to confirm the medication I was on, but I notice she handled my pills. Maybe she was counting them, I am not certain.

I bring this up with LyRae, and she got the same vibe from her. We reached a conclusion that she just was not a friendly person, just maybe a little socially awkward. What happened was, she came and sat in the chair next to me. I was not looking at her, but LyRae was. What she saw was the nurse screwing back on the bottle cover. LyRae counted the pills after that nurse left and found that she took nine pills. To be sure, LyRae counts my pills again and confirms my medication herself. She has her own list and her own records. She has been meticulously keeping track of my medication. She notices that some of my pills are missing. She counts them again. The nurse had taken nine pills of my pain medication.

Yes, nine pills were missing. Just the pills, nothing else was missing.

LyRae goes ahead and reports it to their headquarters right away, and they launched an investigation. A manager and a director came to our home to interview us that same afternoon. They mostly talked to LyRae. The following week, a new nurse came in. I do not know what happened to that other one who stole my pills. She never came back, and I do not spend time thinking about this too much. Perhaps she needed them at that time more than I?

My PT sessions continue two or three times a week. I like this therapist. She is very friendly. They sent us Rachel. She is very clean and hygienic. Whenever she arrived, she would start by spreading her napkin and sanitize everything before she uses them.

"I do this all the time, at every session, with every patient," she tells me.

"That is a very good practice."

"Yes, hygiene is very important," she says.

"Indeed it is!" I respond.

"Shall we begin?" she asks.

"Let's do it. I am ready!" I say enthusiastically.

She comes in twice a week and always leaves me instructions for the days that she is not around. She asks me to stand by the wall or a chair, or near the island in the kitchen. She asks me to stoop down like I am picking something up, basically exercises that strengthen my muscles because they are still weak. I am excited to finally be able to get rid of the cane and finally start moving around without it. Rachel says I am getting close to being able to do that.

The small goals I have set for myself are what keeps me going. They are small goals that lead to much larger goals. First, I must get rid of the cane. I should not need it after another week.

Rachel suggested that I put a bar right next to my bed, for when I have to get up from lying down. It is the hardest position to get up from. The support will be a tremendous help, she said. LyRae and I got one, as suggested, and Rachel was right! I can get up from bed much easier with the support.

Every day, small things are a little easier to do. Getting up, for one, is easier with the bar. Walking around is easier the more I do it. I start taking longer walks around the community, and I start going alone, finally! I go alone, but I go slowly. No reason to rush or to stress myself out. I am getting where I need to be, and it feels good.

After two weeks Dr. Burkhart clears me. I now go to another doctor. She was the gastroenterologist I saw upon my arrival at Duke University Hospital. My case was assigned to her, Dr. Shelby, a sweet and awesome doctor. I will be going to her for my follow-ups for the remainder of the year. I also meet with Teresa, my new transplant coordinator regularly. She is a very nice, amiable woman. I cannot help but think about Cristina, not to compare, but that woman left quite an impression, and she helped out a lot, as I remember it.

Things are much clearer now, much clearer than ever.

Memories of what happened to me start coming back.

There are some things that I find out in my conversations with LyRae. Some of them I remember; some of them I still do not. But I feel more like myself than I have in the past few weeks. The memories feel like they are scrambled and are just now coming back.

I still cannot believe I had a liver transplant. It is so unreal. Nobody can tell me what happened during my surgery. I am sure my surgeon will be happy to, but I do not think I will ever be satisfied with whatever he will tell me. I decide to watch a liver transplant surgery online so that I have an idea.

It is truly shocking.

They opened me up, quite literally. They sliced right through my skin, across the middle, stretched my skin from top to bottom, and clamped it. Unconsciously, I touch my scar. I did not realize how stretchable the skin is.

All my organs were all there, exposed. Neatly arranged, each beating and alive, fulfilling its purpose. Except for the liver, of course. I discover that to get to it, they had to move all my other organs around.

They had carefully, steadily detached my liver from the rest of my body, detached from the major arteries, detached from my veins. My surgery was seven hours plus, with no complications. The detaching takes a bit of time, so does the reattachment.

They waited for the new liver to respond and work with the rest of my body. They waited for it to turn a certain shade of color, and when it did, I guess that is when they closed me back up. The video was quite graphic. I am not even sure I would watch it again.

I go back to the hospital to get a CT scan. Dr. Shelby wanted to check for liver cancer. This was one of the things they said they needed to look out for. I did the CT scan in the same hospital. The preliminary results show that there is no cancer. This is great news. It will take a couple of days for the final results.

It is still early, so LyRae shows me where the ICU is. It is in the same area. It feels odd. I know I spent some time here, but I barely recognize the place.

The charge nurse on the floor sees me, and she recognizes me!

"Hey, I know you. You were just in here!" she says, surprised.

She looks vaguely familiar. I would be lying if I said I remember her clearly.

"You were in this room right here! Come, let me show you. And you know what, I did not realize you were so tall!" she says as she waves her hand, a gesture telling us to follow.

LyRae tells me that the hospital is very strict about the people they let in that particular area, so we look at each other, and together, we shrug our shoulders and follow the nurse.

I wanted to see my room.

"This was the room you were in," she says as she stops.

I cannot look, see, or go inside the room itself. It is occupied. I see the structure. It does look familiar, but I do not remember it very clearly. I recognize the shelves, maybe? I do remember the number 7 vividly. This is definitely my room.

It has been an interesting day. I wait for more memories to come back, but that was it for now. Maybe they will turn up later on, who knows? For now, I still cannot grasp the magnitude of my sickness. All I know is I was really sick. I do not even know what that means. I cannot imagine it. It is hard to picture this.

In my next doctor's visit, we went through my normal routine. Checking my incision, talking about my diet, and Dr. Shelby ruled out liver cancer after seeing my CT scan. This visit, although normal, is a special one. I am able to arrange a meeting, one that I have always wanted to arrange, but never got a chance until today. I have a meeting with Cristina Sung. Before that though, I meet with Teresa first, as I always do when I visit the clinic and I tell her, "You know, people continue to tell me that I was very sick."

"You were," she responds immediately.

"Yes, I understand, but somehow I cannot grasp it. That does not mean anything to me. I cannot put it in any sort of context. I do not know what very sick really means when people say it to me."

Teresa pauses to think that over. "In your time in the ICU, before your transplant," she starts to say.

"Yes?" I say, riveted.

"That was a Sunday to Thursday. You were in the ICU. You were down to a 1 percent chance of survival," she says and pauses, waiting for my reaction.

One percent.

I sit there, stunned, in complete disbelief.

"One percent?" I whisper to myself. "Really, just 1 percent?" I ask her.

"That is all you had," she replies.

"Everyone was nervous about your surgery. Normally, they would not have taken anyone into surgery with those kinds of chances," she continues.

"Why did they?" I wonder.

"It was Dr. Burkhart. He really believed you needed that liver. He was determined to give you one. He said those exact words too. He said, 'I am doing this surgery because this man needs a liver immediately.'"

I do not know what to say, I fall silent.

Teresa continues, "The only way he was not going to do the surgery was if you died on the way to surgery or once you were placed on the table."

"But I did not," I say, trailing off.

"No, you did not. You are a fighter, Mr. Thompson," Teresa says. "Your chances were so slim. There was even a designated back-up patient already, in case you did not make it. The liver would then go to that patient."

I am speechless. I asked for context, here it was. It is unbelievable. I have even more gratitude and respect for everyone who took care of me. I want to thank them all. Teresa took myself and LyRae to a different part of Duke Hospital, where I met Cristina Sung.

"Mr. Thompson!" Cristina exclaims as she sees me. "And Mrs. Thompson! How are you two doing?"

"Better than the last time I saw you, Cristina. Thank you for meeting with me. I wanted to thank you for all your help."

"I am happy to help," she says with a grin. "Are you ready for a tour?"

"Yes, I am. Let's do it."

As we turn a corner, I see a familiar man. His stance, the way he moved, is familiar. He looks at me, recognizing me. "Hey, I know you! Mr. Thompson! You look great. How are you? Wow! You are looking really well," he says. "Very happy to see how well you are doing." He was the same nurse who volunteered to take me outside after my operation.

"I am vertical!" I tell him, and we both laugh. "I am glad I ran into you. I wanted to thank you for all your help."

"No one does that, you know," he tells me.

"Does what?"

"Come back just to thank us. I really appreciate it. I kind of have to go though. It is pretty busy around here."

"Sure, do your thing!"

A doctor passes by. "Is that Dr. Burkhart?" I ask Cristina.

"Yes," she replies, waving him over. He starts making his way toward us.

"Well, look who it is! You are looking well, Mr. Thompson," he tells me.

"I would not be here if it was not for your help, Dr. Burkhart. Thank you so much."

"You are welcome. I am just glad to know you are doing better," he tells me sincerely.

I also get a chance to meet and thank Michelle, the social worker who arranged my transfer to rehab, as well as the chief of the gastroenterology department, who was always present during my stay there but I do not quite remember. I also meet Alex and Liz, my OT and PT who helped me after my surgery. Each one of these people tells me that patients do not come back just to thank them and that they appreciate what I am doing. I cannot keep Cristina much longer. LyRae and I thank her again and leave.

I come back home and sit on my couch for a bit.

Whenever I think about the entire thing, I find it so unbelievable still.

I catch myself forgetting and then asking why I am having so much trouble doing normal things.

Why is it so painful to walk?

Why is it so hard to stand up from a sitting position?

Why do I hesitate to pick up the pen I dropped?

Why do I have to rest after just two minutes of standing?

And then it hits me. The liver transplant.

The things that I start to remember make it real.

The pain that I feel when I take a step when I stand from a sitting pose makes it real.

I spent two months in a hospital being poked and prodded, examined and bedridden.

I came home with a new liver.

I came home with one less organ that I do not feel I am missing.

I have been home for eight weeks, and I feel good. I look out, and it is a nice night to go for a walk. Before I leave, I see my cane lying on the floor.

Do I need it?

I smile to myself. *I don't.*

The breeze feels cool on my skin. The weather is warm, and I am a happy man. I breathe it all in and take my first step, each one easier, lighter than the other.

I am forty-nine years old.

I almost died. I looked death in face. My life lied in the balance between life and death, then the grave.

Twice.

I weighed 240 pounds when I started getting sick. I weighed 220 pounds when I was first admitted to the hospital. I came home at 168 pounds.

I am now at 216 pounds with the help and care of my loving family.

I look up at the dark-blue sky and thank God for another chance at life.

I thank God for the things that I have.

What is in store for me next? I do not know, but I am going to find out.

I am sure that God will tell me.

> *My God, my Father in Heaven, the Alpha and the Omega. The beginning and the ending, you are the Great I am. I thank you for this day. I thank you for my life, health, and strength. Lord, you have been so good to me, from the rising of the sun until the closing of the day. I thank you for allowing me to live, move, and have my being. I thank you for salvation. Lord, you Saved me, Sanctified me, and filled me with the Holy Ghost. For all of that, I give you thanks. As I sit and contemplate my life, I am grateful for life itself. Lord, you took me in to the hospital on January 27 with an acute onset of liver failure. While in the hospital you allowed me to withstand my blood pressure dropping to 50/30. In most cases one would have falling into a coma or even died, but you allowed me to be a miracle. After moving from day to day, I watched my life go downhill by the looks on the faces of others around me. For I only had a 1 percent chance to live. However, you allowed me to make it to February 16, and you allowed me to go into surgery for a liver transplant. Through a few ups and downs in the hospital, you allowed me to go to rehab. During my rehab stay I received excellent therapy. I spent three weeks in rehab; but you, oh Lord, discharged me on March 27. Through all my hospital stays, along with rehab, I am grateful for your continual grace and mercy. Now, three years later, you have blessed me with good health and the recovery has been well.*

You have been right there by my side every day. For that I am grateful beyond words. You have been my all and all, and for that I will serve you all the days of my life. Lord, I bless you, I love you, and I thank you. I pray this prayer to you—my Savior, In Jesus name, Amen.

In order to book speaking engagements or receive more information, please contact us at:

www.thompsonlifeline.com

information@thompsonlifeline.com

Telephone Number: 919-617-1741

We would like to thank each and everyone of you for purchasing the book, One Percent. It is our prayer and hope that you enjoyed this book. We hope to provide you with other reading material in the future.

Thank you for your support,

Mrs. LyRae D. Nelson-Thompson

Mr. Ray E. Thompson, Sr.